The Open University
Arts: A Fourth Level Course
Great Britain 1750–1950
Sources and Historiography   Block I Units 1–2

£1·40

Introduction: Sources, Themes and Projects
Prepared by the Course Team

The Open University Press

Contributors to Block I

Arthur Marwick, Professor of History at the Open University
Neil Wynn, formerly Lecturer in History at the Open University
now Lecturer in History at Glamorgan Polytechnic
Bernard Waites, Research Assistant in History at the Open
University
John Golby, Staff Tutor in History, the Open University,
Southern Region
Clive Emsley, Lecturer in History at the Open University
Gillian Kay, Staff Tutor in History, the Open University in
Northern Ireland
Ian Donnachie, Staff Tutor in History, the Open University
in Scotland
Christopher Harvie, Lecturer in History at the Open University
Anthony Coulson, the Open University Library

CC

The Open University Press,
Walton Hall, Milton Keynes.

First published 1974.

Designed by the Media Development Group of the Open
University.

Printed in Great Britain by
Martin Cadbury, a specialized division of Santype International,
Worcester and London.

ISBN 0 335 00950 6

This text forms part of an Open University course. The complete
list of units in the course appears at the end of this text.

For general availability of supporting material referred to in this
text, please write to the Director of Marketing, The Open
University, P.O. Box 81, Walton Hall, Milton Keynes, MK7
6AT.

Further information on Open University courses may be
obtained from the Admissions Office, The Open University,
P.O. Box 48, Walton Hall, Milton Keynes, MK7 6AB.

1.1

Contents

Paper 1: Themes and Projects

Arthur Marwick

The Ethos of the Course

As a Fourth Level Course *Great Britain 1750–1950: Sources and Historiography* departs radically both in content, and above all in presentation, from all previous Arts Faculty and history courses. Here you will not find the structured 'tutorial in print' method which we developed for the earlier levels. That is not to say, however, that it has not been planned with the same care that we put into all of our courses; indeed it has been deliberately conceived as the culmination of the particular work which, within the general field of the Humanities, you have been doing in history. As you know, up to half of your work will be concerned with a private research project for which direct guidance will come from your tutor; we can only give more generalized help through the correspondence material, television and radio. Though I continue to believe very strongly that no course can be properly taught unless those teaching it have a clear idea of what it is they are setting out to achieve, I do not feel that it is quite appropriate in this instance to keep spelling out objectives in the way we have done in the past. In a moment I shall give some general aims, and a definition of the tasks which we shall expect you to be able to perform, but first I should like to stress what I call the 'ethos' of the course. A university should always, in some sense, be a cooperative venture between staff and students. Obviously, in earlier years there is a very real sense in which 'we' are teaching 'you'. Now, in this final year I should very much like to feel that the whole ethos or atmosphere is one of joint endeavour; we are *together* exploring new areas of historical study and research. Of course, in the end the situation must remain that of, as it were, 'master' and 'apprentice': in other words, though I wish to stress the cooperative nature of the enterprise, that does not in any way absolve us from giving you the necessary guidance to enable you to get on with your work. But, once again, that guidance will not be of the highly organized and structured nature that we have hitherto provided.

General Aims of the Course

Quite simply, this course aims to build on the historical skills you have already acquired in the previous three levels of work, and while recognizing that the Open University does not provide the opportunity for the extent of geographical and chronological coverage normal in a traditional university, to take you to a level appropriate to a student in his final year of history Honours. In the case of all of you, this should mean that by the end of the course you should be at least as well trained in the fundamental historical skills and concepts as any other honours history graduate; in the case of the most distinguished of you, you should be fully equipped to embark upon postgraduate work in history. (You will, at the same time, have the enormous advantage over other graduates of the breadth in other disciplines provided by the Open University curriculum.)

Previously, I have suggested that the historian's activities can be reduced to four. First, he must go out and find his material. Secondly, he must bring to bear on that material the historical techniques of source criticism, aided by the knowledge he already has of his subject from his study in other relevant source materials. Out of this, thirdly, he produces an interpretation. Fourthly, the historian must communicate that interpretation to others. However, these four activities conceal a considerable range of separate skills; they also presume an understanding of what, in the first place, the study of history is all about. Probably you have developed some clear ideas of your own on this matter since the foundation year, and I certainly don't want to be dogmatic about this now. But perhaps I could just remind you of what, to *me*, are the three basic concerns of the historian:

(i)   man in society;

(ii) change through time (a vital ingredient in history, and one which distinguishes it from the more static studies of the social scientist);

(iii) particular unique events (as opposed, again, to the abstract conceptualizations of the social sciences).

I also stressed in the Foundation Course that history involves *explanation* and the study of the *interconnections* between events; it is not mere narration of events without explanation or interpretation. Now, with particular reference to this course, I should like to stress above all that the competent student of history should be able to establish a balance between detailed study on one limited topic and the broader perspective. In one sense, that is what this whole course is about. With regard to the skills needed, you will by this time be thoroughly aware of the fundamental principles of source criticism. You will be aware, too, of the problems of interpretation, and the pitfalls to be surmounted in writing history. Finally, the study of history, apart from any particular essay or research project one may be engaged on, obviously involves the mastery of a fair amount of factual information, and an understanding 'from the inside', as I sometimes put it, of the whole historical period which one is studying. Let me then say briefly what it is you have to do in this course.

1   You should acquire a general knowledge of the entire period of British *domestic* history from 1750 to 1950, remembering our emphasis on man in society (rather than individual 'great men'), change, and unique historical circumstances (though, of course, we are also interested in the broader patterns of change). You should broadly understand the contributions to historical study made by the authors of the various prescribed texts. (Incidentally, although foreign policy as such is excluded from this course, it would be possible to touch on this, as indeed imperial policy, if you wanted to, treating these topics as the function of particular élites—e.g. of the political élite in general, or of the Foreign Office, or of the ambassadors, etc.)

2   For more specialized knowledge (that is to say, involving some of the primary source material and a detailed knowledge of the main historiographical controversies) you can concentrate either on one of the three themes followed right through the course, or else on all three themes for a period of time equivalent to one-third of the total chronological scope of the course.

3 You must carry through a private research project falling within the period studied and relating to one or more of the themes. You will not write a thesis, but in the final examination you will be given two hours or three hours (the choice is yours) in which to 'discuss your research project, with particular reference to the sources used, with an evaluation of their usefulness or otherwise, the most important discoveries you have made, the problems you have encountered, and the relationship of this project to the broader perspective of the course as a whole'.

The Three Themes

In the end all historical writing, unless it assumes the form of the most tedious 'factual' textbook, is in some sense thematic. Whether he admits it or not, or whether he is even aware of it, the historian necessarily selects certain themes to organize his material around. Two hundred years of recent British history is actually an enormous amount, so we had to be pretty selective in choosing our themes, in order to produce a coherent, manageable course. These particular ones were chosen partly because we want to put the stress on social, rather than on political and constitutional, or even economic, history, and to direct attention towards the sort of questions we feel historians ought to be asking; and partly, therefore, because these themes give rise to all sorts of interesting ideas for private research projects.

I want here briefly to give my interpretation and discussion of each of these themes in turn; at the end of this paper my colleagues will have the opportunity to comment and elaborate on my definitions. The themes are 'Poverty and Social Policy'; 'Popular Politics'; and 'Élites'. It cannot be too strongly stressed that these, obviously, are not mutually exclusive compartments. The very overlap involved is highly fruitful in bringing out the vital point that what is often so critical in historical study is the questions you ask, or even the way in which you formulate a question. Slightly different questions asked of the same material will often produce excitingly different answers. 'Poverty and Social Policy' is almost a double topic anyway, and clearly it is perfectly true that often social policy is the direct product of action taken by a political élite, or a product of pressure engendered by popular politics. But there is a difference of orientation. When talking about 'poverty and social policy' one is essentially interested in social policy in connection with its actual effects on the conditions of the poor; one is interested in the results of social policy. If social policy were considered under either of the other two headings, one would then be showing an interest in its causes rather than its results.

Of course, to understand these themes you have to have a broader knowledge of the total history of the period, and, in particular, we have suggested in the Prospectus entry that you should regard economic and technological history as a kind of sub-theme. At the other extreme stands intellectual history, which may not at first sight seem to be at all relevant; but rephrased in the form of 'what ideas were current among certain élite groups at certain points of time' it immediately becomes relevant again. We are not interested in constitutional history as such, but you must have a grasp of the constitutional framework of the country, the nature of local government and so on, if you are to understand the framework in which our various themes operate. Finally, political narrative as such is not what we are interested in: but since our approach is so strongly analytic, you may well find it useful for your own purposes to make some effort to get the political chronology of the period clear, again as a kind of simple frame of reference to operate in.

1 *Poverty and Social Policy.* This was quite definitely meant to be our first theme, though for practical reasons (one of the Course Team members was unavailable in America until September 1973) we do not in fact start the course with this subject. But the basic idea is that this theme firmly directs our attention away from 'minority' towards 'majority history'. One prime concern, at least, of the historian should be with the conditions of the mass of the people. So in studying 'poverty' we ask the basic question, 'What were living conditions like at a particular time in a particular place?' Then we want to ask, 'How far did poverty disappear, and if it did, was this due to social policy, and, further, in what ways did social policy change?' Detailed questions arise, like our old friend 'Did the Industrial Revolution increase or decrease poverty?' There are all sorts of questions about the nature and significance of the welfare state. You can see that this is an extremely rich topic, and should give rise to all sorts of possibilities for local study.

2 *Popular Politics.* Here again we are thinking of 'majority history' as much as of 'minority history'. If we accept that at any point of time in any given society, power, roughly speaking, is monopolized by a certain class or group, or classes and groups, then 'popular politics' broadly covers all attempts by 'outsider' classes and groups to challenge this monopoly. Questions arise about whether the victims of the 'poverty' of our first theme are, at any given point of time, actually politically active, or whether, on closer investigation, 'popular politics' does not often turn out to be largely an activity of richer middle-class elements, or even of rebel members of the ruling class. One major historical question will indeed be that of when, and with what effect, the working-class as such became active in politics.

3 *Élites.* Traditional 'minority history' has tended to concentrate exclusively on the doings of, and the changes brought about, by the powerful minority, without concerning itself over-much with the composition of this minority and the means by which it attained and held power. Clearly the 'minority historians' are absolutely right in insisting on the importance in any society of those who wield power. In studying this theme we want to look at who held power at any particular point in time, how far there were changes in the composition of the groups which held power, and how effective the various ruling groups were. Although the word has a rather different derivation, 'élites', as now used by social scientists and historians, refers to those minorities which are set apart from the rest of society by their pre-eminence in authority, achievement and reward, or any one or two of these. Raymond Aron, the French sociologist, has suggested the following list as being relevant to élites in modern industrial countries: political leaders; administrative leaders; economic leaders; labour leaders; cultural leaders; and military leaders. Apart from the fact that this list is in itself debatable, it must be stressed that we begin our study in pre-industrial Britain, when a totally different list might well seem to be relevant. In fact, one major question underlying the whole

theme is 'How far has industrialization affected the entire nature of élites in British society?' We shall also want to bear in mind a distinction between national élites and local élites. In your own research projects you may well wish to study the élite in one particular local community.

The Research Project

The rationale behind the research project is perfectly simple. It is that you have not properly studied history until you have done some history for yourself. You've had a fair amount of practice up till now in handling printed primary documents; now is the time to get out amongst the real thing for yourself. Remember, of course, that this is not comparable to a three or four years' full-time Ph.D. project: you should not spend on the research project more than half the time you have at your disposal for this entire course; and, unlike a Ph.D. thesis where you are pretty well your own master, you have still to show in this project that you can relate your detailed work to the broader perspective of the course. It is certainly not open to you to pursue a piece of research which has absolutely no relationship at all to the course as a whole.

Most of you, I fancy, will find your project in some branch of local history, and, in the main, I should think that this is the most rewarding kind of research for you to do.

It would be possible from sources which are printed, and available in the larger libraries, but which are nonetheless unimpeachably primary sources, to work on a national rather than a local theme. One way in here is to consider studying 'attitudes': attitudes towards poverty, or social policy, or even towards élites. A starting-point for the last topic might be two books by the Liberal intellectual C. F. G. Masterman, *The Condition of England*, which he published in 1910, and *England After the War* which he published in 1922. These books express very strong views on the class structure and the power structure in Britain at two points in time. If you could track down other such works, and also statements in novels and so on, you could write a study on, say, 'Changing Attitudes towards the Aristocracy 1900–1930', or something like that. Large libraries have volumes of Parliamentary Papers, reports of learned societies, Labour Party and Trade Union Annual Reports, periodicals and newspapers. From these, and from published reminiscences and diaries, it is also possible to do limited research projects of considerable value. For instance, one might simply study the report of one Royal Commission in detail, using the report itself in the bound volumes of Parliamentary Papers, tracking down through parliamentary debates and newspapers the process by which the Commission was set up (you would need private papers of course to get at the detailed story, but in your sort of project that wouldn't necessarily be needed). You could use the biographical dictionaries, biographies and autobiographies, to compile some detail on the various members of the Commission, and you could attempt to assess the consequences of their labours. Some libraries have special collections of certain types of political pamphlet: the existence of such a collection might immediately suggest a viable topic.

For the more likely local research project, my colleagues will be offering detailed suggestions. The sorts of thing I have always had in mind are for example: to take a parti-

cular community over a particular period of time, say ten years, and try to pin down exactly who were the dominant people ('the élite') in that particular community; or to take a particular piece of national legislation, and see how it actually panned out in a particular locality—the Local Government Act of 1929, for instance, the old and the new Poor Law, and also subsequent pieces of social legislation, provide lots of scope for the study of local implications. If you happen to have strong connections with a particular school, whether in the 'poverty' or 'élite' class, it might be very valuable to try to track down the subsequent career patterns of some of its pupils. That sort of topic, and many other semi-biographical topics, are often easier for the modern period, where you can still get in touch with the people themselves or their immediate heirs. On popular politics there is a whole range of Labour and Trade Union activity at the local level: you might also consider such other 'outsider', but now fashionable, groups as women and young people. Whatever you do, will necessarily depend on there being available accessible source materials. But remember too that it is vital to be always asking questions: if, say, there is a general theory that sometime in the early twentieth century aristocratic rule in the rural areas gave way to professional local authority rule, you could try to check whether this theory is borne out by an actual piece of local experience.

The Nature of the Correspondence Material

For this course, as distinct from all its predecessors, the correspondence material simply takes the form of a series of papers of the sort which we might read if we had a group of final year history students together in a seminar. Sometimes these papers will be followed by separate comments and criticisms by other members of the Course Team. Most of them will be fairly closely related to the major historical works which are set as part of your prescribed reading. Others, particularly at the beginning of the course, are designed to help you with getting on with your own research project. There will be no questions and exercises directed straight at you. It is for you now to think out questions to ask yourself, and for you to resolve, or reject, the various different interpretations which you will encounter in the course. Since these 'seminar papers' are designed to illuminate specific topics, or to stimulate discussion, and do not, therefore, provide any full coverage of the period from 1750 to 1950, it is all the more essential that you should have a reliable textbook to provide this necessary background information for you. Now no history book, as you know, is definitive; all history books in the end are one man's interpretation. Let me therefore look more closely for a moment at R. K. Webb's *Modern England*, and suggest some ways in which you can make use of this book. You will indeed need to make constant and extensive use of it; but you must, naturally, in no circumstances come to regard it as any kind of 'Bible'.

'Modern England from the Eighteenth Century to the Present'

R. K. Webb, Allen and Unwin, 1969.

Robert K. Webb is a distinguished American authority (hence the American spellings) on modern British history. His most detailed work has been done on the early nineteenth century, and he has made particularly original and valuable studies of a vital, but previously much neglected topic, the extent of working-class literacy in the nineteenth century. You can take it that Webb's is no casual outsider's view. He has, as all historians must, deeply immersed himself in British history; and his work is thoroughly authoritative in the sense that he has mastered all the latest research by other specialist historians. At the same time, because he is an American, he has gone back to first principles in a way in which many native British historians would not do. I particularly commend Appendices 2, 3 and 4, which you might profitably read before ever you embark on the book itself as he himself suggests.

I shall leave you to form your own opinions, should you feel this to be particularly relevant, on Webb's political attitudes and general outlook. I should say that, in keeping with what can be called the modern professional or empirical approach, these do not obtrude very much. Webb could perhaps be characterized as an American Liberal intellectual who takes a commonsense, no nonsense approach to the sentimentalities and myths of British history. For example, we see something of the rugged, private enterprise outlook when Webb, writing about the Industrial Revolution, says (p. 117) that low wages and long hours 'did not seem unjust to the entrepreneur, who himself might well work sixteen or eighteen hours a day managing the plant'. On the other hand the American Liberal shines through when, speaking of George III's condemnation of Pitt's proposal for Catholic Emancipation as 'the most Jacobinical thing I ever heard of!' Webb remarks (p. 138), 'we may fairly conclude that he was demonstrating the muddled thinking as typical of the late eighteenth-century gentlemen as the slovenly use of "communist" has become of a good many of their twentieth-century counterparts'. More to the point, perhaps, is Webb's sober professional conservatism, almost Rankean in tone, which insists on seeing each age on its own terms, and rejects the notion that you can criticize people for not thinking of reforms which did not in fact come about till a later period. Speaking of the criticisms that have been made of the Poor Law commissioners of 1834, Webb remarks (p. 245) that 'it is hard to know what practical remedies they could have suggested at the time for the more fundamental causes of poverty, the solution to which had to await a further stage in industrial and administrative growth'. On the whole Webb seems to be keen to play down the influence of the guided action of individuals. He says (rightly, most historians would now agree) that the Anti-Corn Law League 'did not convert Peel or Parliament; protection was struck down through the votes of men persuaded by events and economic logic' (p. 270). However, in discussing the social policy of the Edwardian period he remarks (p. 456): 'There was nothing automatic about social reform, even when the ground was well prepared; to enact it required stamina, authority, and egotism.' Here we are at one of the central questions in historical study: how much weight, in any particular case, do we give to the 'logic of events', how much to the actions of individuals?

In my view, the cautious, sceptical, 'professional' approach adopted by Webb is one of the major keys to its success as a textbook. What you get, in the main, is a clear presentation of the latest research on the various major topics, in which Webb admits to the complexities of the problems involved, rather than giving a simplified view which inclines in the direction of one orthodoxy or another. Perhaps the finest example of all in the entire book is the discussion of the Reform Act of 1832 and the question of the middle classes in the bottom half of page 218. Much the same can be said of the discussion of Chartism at the bottom of page 248 (though it is my own view that Webb does not quite fully understand Chartism on its own terms, nor the problems with which it had to contend). From page 48 onwards there is an excellent summary of the interpretation of eighteenth-century politics created by Sir Lewis Namier (though again one might possibly argue that too little attention has been paid to the later critics of Namier), and you get a marvellously unromantic view of John Wilkes (p. 76). This is in no way to suggest that Webb's book is merely a non-committal digest of the latest accepted views. On the contrary, the book frequently prefers to raise, rather than attempt to answer, questions. There are many interesting generalizations and aphorisms, such as the ones on the Anti-Corn Law League or Edwardian social reform I have already quoted, which you should use as a basis for further thought and exploration.

There are two other aspects of the book which I particularly admire. The first I have already touched on in regard to the appendices to the book. This is Webb's habit of getting down to the concrete detail, of telling us the simple things we need to know, but which writers of historical works so often ignore. It's good to know the exact origin and meaning of such terms as 'First Lord of the Treasury' and of such common words as 'mob'; it's good to be told just how exactly Huskisson came to be killed by that train; and it is interesting, and in this particular case relevant, to know that distinguished visitors in the nineteenth century were always taken on a tour of Barclay's Brewery (page 275, footnote). Webb points out at the foot of page 38 that the famous Dissenting Academies were short-lived; I can remember as a student being very puzzled because nobody told me what had happened to these apparently so celebrated institutions.

The other important strength is Webb's grasp of the significance of geography and the landscape: it is with this that the book begins, and geography forms a kind of basic theme, touched on again, brilliantly, for example on page 264. At a more fundamental level, of course, the book is a useful simple guide to other secondary authorities: it is your job here to pay close attention to the footnotes. On page 223, for example, there is a short but very useful list of key works on local government history. Obviously, bibliographical information quickly falls out of date, and since Webb went to press more work on nineteenth-century Trade Unions has appeared than he allows for in his footnote on page 238. A later paper in this course by Clive Emsley updates and improves upon the views presented in the second footnote on page 157.

Obviously, no historical work, particularly one of this size and scope, is without faults. As some of you probably know, I always react particularly strongly against such vague, imprecise phrases as 'the national mood' (page 73) or 'the country sensed a change' (page 164): in my view Webb is much too free with such phrases, though interestingly he becomes much more precise when he is trying to do the same kind of thing in the twentieth century part of the book. Most of the minor points which I think Webb has got wrong (mainly, be it said, because of the need to condense) are not relevant to the major themes which you are studying. However, in case you are interested in popular politics in the 1930s, you might, for example, note that the reference to the East Fulham by-election on page 529 is rather inaccurate: the election was very largely fought on domestic issues, particularly housing, and the Labour candidate, far from being a 'pacifist', claimed to be a supporter of collective security through the League of Nations. (This, incidentally, is a perfect example of the sort of local study you could do to examine in detail the sort of statements you get in a general textbook like Webb's.) Right at the very beginning of the book there seems to me to be a confusing contradiction between page 7, where Webb seems to be saying that there was a gulf between the aristocracy and the commoners (including baronets and knights) and page 11 where, rightly I think, he says there were strong characteristics binding all landed gentry together. Furthermore, again rightly I think, he stresses on page 13 that there was much less of a distinction between landed society and the world of business than there was in Continental countries. I don't want by any means to suggest that Webb is not worth paying attention to on working-class history: but this is perhaps a particular area where further reading and research of your own may well qualify some of the views expressed by Webb. I find it significant that on page 393, in a footnote reference to one of the books we have set you as prescribed reading, Henry Pelling's *The Origins of the Labour Party*, he merely refers to this as 'a general account of political labour', completely missing the point that this, at the time of publication, was a highly original work which altered many of the fashionable views about the origins of the Labour Party. (This is why it is one of your set books.) In particular, Henry Pelling suggested that the Fabian Society had played a less crucial role in the founding of the Labour Party than had formerly been believed; Webb, in my view, continues in later passages of the book to slightly overrate the significance of the Fabian Society.

You will have appreciated just how important Webb is to you in this course, as the only means of acquiring an overall coverage of the period to be studied. It will be especially important if you have no previous general knowledge of the period, or, equally, if your knowledge of the period dates back to something you learned a decade or more ago; if you find what Webb says is in sharp conflict with your own previously held ideas, please do believe that Webb is much more in touch with up-to-date scholarship than whoever taught you in the past can possibly have been. You have had enough experience of University work now to be able to work out for yourself the best means of using Webb. Here, however, are some tentative suggestions of my own as to the sort of very broad general questions you might have in mind when reading the book. First of all, since I have already suggested that you may well find it useful to try to get a kind of chronological frame of reference for the entire period fixed in your mind, you might examine the way in which Webb divides the whole time-span of his book into shorter chronological periods. As you can readily see from the table of contents, he makes four major chronological divisions; then within that he breaks political history (not our basic concern in this course) down into shorter periods, with other

chapters discussing special topics, and therefore breaking across the political chronology. You could compare Webb's periodization with that of the only other book prescribed which covers such a long span of time, Derek Fraser's *Evolution of the British Welfare State*, or indeed with any other reputable general textbook. I don't want to put too much stress on this. Remember that periods are simply labels invented by historians (note, incidentally, what Webb says about this, particularly on page 486). All I am saying is that you will almost certainly find it valuable to have a chronological framework in mind, though you must always accept that any such framework is open to modification and qualification, and certainly has no inherent absolute validity. Secondly, you should be constantly asking yourselves what relationship there is between what Webb is saying and your three main themes of study. Thirdly, you should be constantly on the look out for generalizations or questions which you feel call for further exploration, either at a fairly general level in the secondary sources, or perhaps even as the basis for your own specialized research project. Beyond that, you can always keep yourself alert by raising all the sorts of questions about Webb's strengths and weaknesses as a historian which I have already briefly touched on. Finally, be sure not to miss the flashes of real wit which illuminate the book from time to time.

Let me then attempt a few brief pointers as to how you might approach the question of the relationship between what Webb says and your own three main themes for study. Practically none of the book is totally irrelevant, since you need, as we have seen, to get an overall framework. Other parts of the book will be necessary to get a particular frame, the framework of local government for instance, within which a particular theme can be seen to operate. Still other parts of the book will be dealing simultaneously, as it were, with more than one of the themes. I have annotated my copy of Webb all the way through. Now I'm going to run quickly through the book, just mentioning one or two of the marginal notes which I have made on this question. Obviously, from the foot of page 6, and for the next few pages, we are learning a good deal about the nature of élites in Britain around 1750. Note the suggestion towards the foot of page 26 that prior to 1760 there really wasn't anything which could effectively be called 'popular politics' (this is a generalization that needs examining; if there was a change after 1760, this needs explaining). On page 27 we move properly into the area of 'poverty and social politics' with the emphasis mainly on poverty; but note that on the middle of page 29 we are brought back to the question of the absence of popular politics, and that by the foot of the page we are touching on the question of actions and attitudes of the élites ('men of high position'). On page 32 we move away from our themes, yet, as I have already remarked, just as we cannot really comprehend them fully without an understanding of the basic economic and technological history of the period, so too we need to know something about religious and intellectual attitudes. Note the discussion on page 37 of the way in which the Anglican Church meshed into the structure of élites, both national and local. Of the many references to the development of popular politics in the later eighteenth century I noted, among others, pages 91–4 and pages 134–5. What I think Webb handles very well—a simple point, but one not always made in the past—is the distinction between what, briefly,

I shall call middle-class popular activity, and working-class popular activity. The second type of popular politics is of course closely intertwined with the theme of poverty and social policy, as for instance on page 146; then on page 147 we move back into the realm of middle-class popular politics. On page 177 we are told that Lord Grey's son-in-law, John George Lambton, possessed a great fortune founded on coal mines. This whole question of where people's money came from is crucial in the study of élites. And remember, too, in this part of the book that when you are reading about, for example, the Corn Laws, then you are also reading about the attitudes and policies of the ruling élite. Similarly, when on page 180 we are apparently dealing with intellectual history, the discussion of utilitarianism, of course, takes us straight back into the theme of social policy. The discussion of parliamentary reform (page 195) and municipal reform (page 221) again show Webb at his best, and a mastery of this will be vital to you in any study of popular politics in this period. With regard to the source materials for a local topic within the poverty and social policy theme note Webb's point on page 226 about the supersession of the old, rather inefficient parish registers, by new civil registers. On page 229 Webb mentions the way in which the church élite is beginning to move towards becoming a separate and distinct élite, rather than one bound into the fabric of the ruling class as it had been in the eighteenth century. Most of the religious history on the next few pages, though, is of very little relevance to our main themes of study. The pages from 233–42 bring out very nicely the way in which questions of poverty merge into questions of social policy, which in turn merge into questions of popular politics, and back into questions of social policy. Such foreign and colonial policy sections as those covering pages 296–312 are not very directly relevant, unless you are interested in foreign and colonial policy as reflecting attitudes of political élites; or in the attitudes of representatives of popular politics to these topics. On the other hand the economic survey covering pages 369–79 is of absolutely central importance in discussing the relationship of ruling élites to changing industrial and agricultural conditions. Jumping now right over all the dozens of marginal annotations I have in my copy of Webb, let me take a couple of final allusions to élites in the twentieth century (a topic which I shall be discussing more fully right at the end of the course): at the top of page 500 we get a reflection on the *competence* of the British business élite, and at the foot of page 502 we get the suggestion that the politicial élite is being invaded by 'obscure' men. Both of these, perhaps rather banal judgements, could well be subjected to fuller analysis.

The purpose of that quick flick through some of the pages of Webb is to try to suggest to you how you can make use of some of the information in *Modern England*, from the point of view of the three themes we are studying. You will, obviously, not necessarily always want to agree fully with, or accept unquestioningly, the points made by Webb in regard to the three themes. And in certain particular cases, as I have suggested above, you will find points made, or questions raised, which you will want to explore further for yourselves. Again, it is for you to dig these things out for yourselves: here, again, I just offer a few examples which particularly struck me.

Two phrases early on in the book, both very relevant to our main themes, I thought worth further thought and examination, perhaps in the secondary sources, perhaps even as a basis for your private research project: the first is on page 54, and refers to the social policy of the British ruling élite in the eighteenth century: 'It has been said that these limited purposes reflected an administrative rather than a legislative conception of the state.' The second is on page 60, and speaks entirely for itself: 'One can understand what was happening at the centre of eighteenth-century English government only by first understanding the localities.' Another of Webb's generalizations which would repay further study either at the general, or at the local and particular level, occurs on page 128 where he says: 'Ferment in a society may go on making gradual changes, or it may be suddenly speeded up by some external challenge or catastrophe. The latter happened in England, because of the revolution in France.' Another, and perhaps even broader topic for possible exploration, arises from comments made by Webb on pages 294–6, 511 and 538. The questions which arise (remember that in origins Webb is himself essentially an intellectual historian) are: Can one speak of an 'intellectual élite'? What power or influence did this élite have? Did it have a lot of power in the nineteenth century and much less power in the twentieth century? My attention, I should say, has been specially directed towards this topic through discussions with Christopher Harvie, who is an authority on the university intellectuals in the nineteenth century, and who, with me, will be providing most of the material on élites at the end of our period for study. It is on the whole my view that, whatever the situation in the nineteenth century, the professional 'intellectual' class has not had a great deal of influence in the twentieth century. Within this broad topic there ought to be scope for a number of limited private research projects. Finally, I found my interest specially aroused by what Webb says between pages 402 and 404 about the middle classes coming 'fully into their own' in the late nineteenth century and early twentieth century. But does the middle class ever really become a ruling class? Is it not just that the ruling class modifies itself slightly, maintaining a situation in which there is still a recognizable middle class without any real political or economic power? I put this as a question, not as a dogma.

Now to possible research projects, though my aim is not so much to suggest definite titles, as to show you the way in which you might use Webb to work towards arriving at titles for yourselves. At the foot of page 118 Webb mentions the fact that 'the reign of George III saw the multiplication in provincial towns of a curious assortment of institutions', including Improvement Commissioners, Sewer Authorities, and Literary and Philosophical Societies.' He gives a few bare bibliographical references. Here anyway is a potentially fruitful field for local study, linking the theme of the local élite to the theme of social policy. On a number of occasions (for instance on page 236) Webb refers to 'the national vice of drunkenness'. You might well try to find out whether this generalization is accurate for your own particular community; you might study local attempts at temperance reform. On page 247 Webb cites a famous article by Asa Briggs on 'The Language of Class': using Briggs as a model you could either do a local study, or a wider more national study based on a later chronological period. A local study of professional football (page 380) would be an acceptable study within the theme of poverty, broadly conceived. Local trades councils, or other labour bodies, I have already mentioned as possible fields for research; local branches of the Fabian Society (p. 390) or of the WEA (p. 552) might also be suitable. There is still much scope for local study of the labour unrest of the 1920s (pp. 506, 520–1)—how revolutionary, if at all, was the labour movement? Finally, and highly topically, how about picking up on Webb's references to transport reorganization, the development of the motor-car, and so on (pp. 523 and 547)? How about a study of the building in the inter-war period of a tube extension, or a surburban railway, or of a by-pass road? (Provided always, of course, that any such studies are firmly related to one or more of our themes.)

The Other Set Books

If you have read Webb's footnotes as attentively as you should have done, you will have noticed that he mentions all of your set texts, except Mather and Fraser. Most mentions go to E. P. Thompson, with Namier coming a close second. Anyway, you can take this as some kind of confirmation that these books that we are asking you to read are all classics of historiography. F. C. Mather is not mentioned by name in Webb, but his pioneering essay on a hitherto rather neglected aspect of the discussion of Chartism is to be found in the important collection edited by Asa Briggs, mentioned on page 250. Mather's Historical Association pamphlet is an excellent summary of work by himself and others which links Chartism, as part of our popular politics theme, to the reactions of the ruling élite. Only Derek Fraser is odd man out: his book was not even published when this course material was written, and the book was in fact selected on the basis of the proofs. You should yourselves look out to see what the reviewers say about the *Evolution of the Welfare State* when it appears. We have not selected it as a 'great' book but as a useful one. There are a number of other valuable books along much the same lines, but Fraser's has the extra merit of being the most up to date and, from the point of view of the particular orientation taken by this course, the most comprehensive.

Apart from the references in Webb which indicate their areas of importance all the other authors, except F. M. L. Thompson, are discussed in my *The Nature of History.* F. M. L. Thompson is Professor of History at Bedford College, London a leading economic historian, and an unchallenged authority on the landed aristocracy in the nineteenth century. Namier's book is mainly concerned with the theme of élites but is of some importance too in the study of popular politics. E. P. Thompson is of value to us in both the themes of poverty and social policy (principally poverty) and popular politics. F. M. L. Thompson, obviously, is included as part of our study of élites. Blake is included at the insistence of Christopher Harvie, who argues strongly for the importance of the biographical approach to the study of élites. Mather I have just mentioned, and Pelling I have mentioned earlier for his importance in reinterpreting the origins of the Labour Party. Fraser, of course, is important for the social policy aspect of the poverty and social policy theme. There will be more detailed discussion of these various writers in some of the papers which make up the bulk of the corre-

spondence material, and it may be that my colleagues will now wish to add something more.

Set Book List

Webb, R. K., *Modern England from the Eighteenth Century to the Present.* Allen & Unwin, 1969.

Thompson, E. P., *The Making of the English Working Class.* Penguin, 1970.

Namier, L. B., *The Structure of Politics at the Accession of George III.* Macmillan, 1957.

Thompson, F. M. L., *English Landed Society in the Nineteenth Century.* Routledge, 1971.

Pelling, H., *The Origins of the Labour Party 1880–1900.* Oxford, 1965.

Marshall, T. H., *Social Policy.* Hutchinson, 1970.

Mather, F. C., *Chartism.* Historical Association, 1965.

Blake, Robert, *Disraeli.* Methuen, 1969.

A Note on Popular Politics, 1870-1950

Neil Wynn and Bernard Waites

Because the written section of the course on 'Popular Politics, 1870–1950' will come to you fairly late in the year, a brief introduction now may help you with your choice of, and work on, a research topic.

The first thing to be considered should be the nature of popular politics. Unlike other themes, this one is not a constant factor in history: the extension of the franchise in 1884 and again in 1918 in a sense made all political parties 'popular' and by the end of our period of study it is difficult to draw any distinction between popular politics and the politics of élites. You have to bear in mind, for instance, the fact that the Conservative party has consistently attracted the support of a significant proportion of the working classes. The subject area we have taken is that dealing with the evolution and exchange of political ideas amongst the socially under-privileged and the efforts of members of that group to effect social and political change. Broadly speaking, we are concerned with the division between different sections of the working classes, between those on the left and those more conservative elements.

Central to this is the simultaneous growth and development of the Labour Party and the Trade Union movement, and a great deal has, of course, been written about both subjects and their relation to one another. Your set book, Henry Pelling's *Origins of the Labour Party,* is only one of many works in this field but it is important for its new appraisal of the forces responsible for the birth of an independent parliamentary party. However, Pelling and other writers have been concerned largely with popular politics on a national level: little has been written on local developments and, if you like, the grass roots.[1]

1 Paul Thompson's *Socialists, Liberals and Labour: The Struggle for London, 1885–1914,* Routledge & Kegan Paul, London, 1967, is the one notable exception.

Research into the growth and interaction of local labour and socialist organizations would therefore be both fruitful and exciting and could be related to the national scene. In reading through Pelling's and other authors' books you can pick out places (Bradford, Manchester, Glasgow, for example) which only get a brief mention but which deserve more.

The same applies to the other subjects dealt with under the general heading 'Popular Politics, 1870–1950'. It is often said by historians, for instance, that between the death of Chartism and the birth of Socialism there was little working-class radicalism. Is there local evidence to contradict this view? What happened to the Chartists? What about the Republican movement? In the later periods how wide-spread was the pre-World War I working class unrest? Was Syndicalism the force some historians have suggested? How universal was the Shop Stewards movement? Did workers in different areas react to the Depression in the same way? What happened in local politics during World War II? Organizations outside of the mainstream of politics also need examination at a local level: the Communist Party, the British Union of Fascists, even the suffragette movement. If the working class in your particular locality consistently voted for the Conservative Party then the reasons for this could be fruitfully examined. These, and others, are areas which you could think about and perhaps study in detail.

Paper 2: Some Suggestions on Your Research Project

Clive Emsley and John Golby

The list of research topics that you could follow up in this course is endless, and it is clearly out of the question for us to give you a comprehensive list from which you could select a topic. There are probably those among you who have already decided on an area of research for this course, while there are others who have, as yet, no set plans. What we aim to do here is to make a few suggestions which we hope will help those of you who are still pondering, and to make some suggestions about sources which will be of use to all of you. Much of what we have to say here is common sense and it will appear fairly obvious; we still think it is worth saying it as it is all too easy to miss the obvious. The research interests of both of us lie in the early part of the course and this will be reflected in our suggestions, but it should not be difficult for those of you wishing to work somewhere in the period between 1850 and 1950 to follow through our suggestions into that later period of the course.

Probably your research topic will require you to investigate primary sources in local Record Offices. Later on in this block Anthony Coulson will be disussing this kind of source in detail. It is essential, however, that before you plunge into primary sources you have a good grasp of the relevant secondary sources. This will enable you to see your primary material in a wide context, and will also probably enable you to understand much of the evidence in the primary sources with more facility. R. K. Webb and your other set books will obviously be of use to you as secondary material, but it may also be worth your while to consult a bibliography. One of the small Historical Associa-

tion pamphlets, *British History since 1760: a select bibliography* by Ian R. Christie (1970) or *British History since 1926* by C. L. Mowat (1960), would probably serve your purpose for this course; if not, they point the way to the comprehensive bibliographical works that you can follow up.

If your topic is firmly rooted in local history make sure that you are aware of the publications of local history societies in your area, and work through their past volumes. Probably you will find a predilection among contributors in the early part of this century for medieval monastic communities or medieval corporate charters, but don't let that mislead you about some of the later contributions. Similarly, don't be misled by the inclusion of the word 'archaeological' in the title of some of these societies. The *Victoria County Histories* may also be of use to you. Unfortunately the earlier volumes take little cognizance of the period of this course and still less of the three central themes of the course, but those volumes published since the *V.C.H.* came under the auspices of the Institute of Historical Research will probably be of value to you. Another fairly obvious point, if you are working on local history: make sure that you are aware of histories of your town or county as they may have a lot to say about your topic and they may save you a lot of work.

Local Directories, which can often be found in local libraries, are useful in providing information about the towns and villages in your area. The names of the principal inhabitants and leading tradesmen are often included as well as figures giving the size of the village or town. In addition, parish registers of baptisms, marriages and burials and census returns, especially those for 1841 and 1851, can be of immense value in a variety of ways but especially for those people working on population trends, the social composition of a locality and the mobility of the inhabitants in a specific area. The census returns for 1851 record not only every household and the names, ages and occupations of the members of each household, but in addition, give the place of birth of everybody listed in the census. If you are interested in using censuses do look at M. W. Beresford *The Unprinted Census Returns of 1841, 1851, 1861 for England Wales* (Phillimores Handbooks, 1966). This book attempts to show how a social history of a locality can be written using the census as the main documentary source.

During your research you may have cause to consult past runs of newspapers. If your project comes into the early part of the course you will probably find newspapers a disappointing source; they were thin on the ground and provincial papers often lifted passages verbatim from the London papers; your local library, even if it has a collection of eighteenth- and early nineteenth-century papers, may have incomplete runs. Make sure you are aware of the politics of each of the newspapers you handle; the politics of a newspaper are likely to bias its accounts of proceedings, particularly when it comes to popular politics. A study of the politics, attitudes and influence of a local newspaper would, in itself, make an interesting research topic coming into any one of the three themes of the course. There are two valuable monographs relating to this topic in the early part of the course which you may wish to follow up: A. Aspinall, *Politics and the Press, 1780–1850* (1949), and Donald Read, *Press and People, 1790–1850* (1960).

Popular Politics

Historical evidence is always fragmentary; for a subject like popular politics the evidence is more fragmentary than for many others. The members of popular political societies and trade unions have left little in the way of private papers. The people who participated in more primitive forms of social protest (enclosure riots, provision riots, the 'Swing' riots of 1830) left even less. Furthermore, in the early period of the course the popular politics themselves are fragmentary—Luddism, for example, was not something which affected the whole country, and if you have set your mind on a study of Luddism anywhere other than Nottinghamshire, Derbyshire, Leicestershire, Cheshire, Lancashire or Yorkshire, you had better think again.

Probably most of the references to primary sources that you will see in your set books are to collections in London. Obviously, we don't expect you all to travel to London to work in the Public Record Office or the British Museum. It should be possible for you to work up a popular politics project from secondary sources for the general context, and from local newspapers, the private papers of gentlemen, businessmen and any other interested parties which are now collected in your local Record Office. Then there are official papers; for the early period of the course, for example, you could study the records of the Quarter Sessions for the treatment meted out to rioters, strikers and any men charged with uttering seditious expressions, printed or spoken, and the incidence of such crimes. (Of course, you could use these same papers for a totally different kind of topic under the heading of élites: How did any élite of country gentlemen run a county, or how did the élite of a corporate town run that town? It has been argued that the period from 1770 to 1830 saw an enormous increase in the work of the Quarter Sessions; you could test that argument for your own particular area.)

The topics within the popular politics field are many and varied. It would be possible to study a national phenomenon from a local standpoint: Chartism, for example, or the General Strike of 1926. Alternatively, you could study one type of popular politics over a given period of years; the incidence of popular disorder in the late eighteenth or early nineteenth centuries, or trade union activity at a later date. The reactions of governing or business groups (and remember that probably most of your evidence on popular politics will come from the papers of people in these groups) towards types of popular politics over a given period would also make a fruitful line of enquiry. Again, your locality may have a specific incident in its history worth studying (the Leeds municipal strike of 1913, for example) though, of course, you could not afford to study such a topic in complete isolation from the national context.

Finally, parliamentary elections are another source for study. In addition to the sources already mentioned you may find in pamphlet form in your local library or Record Office, speeches, election addresses, posters and accounts of specific elections in the county or in the local parliamentary borough. Another very useful source in studying parliamentary elections is poll-books. These books vary in the amount of information they provide. Some merely contain a list of voters and state for which candidate or candidates they voted. Others give the electors' addresses and some provide the occupations of the electors. Unfortunately poll-books were not produced for each constituency at every election. It has been estimated that about 1750 poll-books were published for different elections in England and Wales during the period 1694 to 1872, and that the details of one-third to one-half of all contested elections between 1832 and 1872 were published in poll-books. (Again, poll-books can be found in your Record Office and, if you are lucky, some borough and county libraries possess copies.)

One word of advice—before using poll-books have a look at J. R. Vincent's *Pollbooks: How Victorians Voted* (Cambridge 1967). The introduction to this book has useful sections on the 'Nature of Pollbooks', 'Problems they can and cannot solve' and 'The interpretation of the data they provide'.

British Elites

Parliamentary elections come under the heading of British Elites as well as Popular Politics. You may wish to examine the machinery and activities of one of the political parties in a particular constituency, or make a study of a particular local MP in order to discover what were his relations with his party and how much he represented the views of his constituents. If you are studying political élites in the eighteenth or nineteenth centuries, a number of questions concerning influence and electioneering are well worth following up. How much influence did the MP exert in his constituency? Did he have commercial or industrial interests or was he a local landowner? How did he exert his influence? Was it by bribery, threats or more subtle means? Or did the constituents vote for him out of personal respect or because of his political allegiances?

The role of the landowner in the local community is another research project worth exploring. We have already mentioned the sort of possible projects in this area that can be envisaged by working on Quarter Session reports, but if you decide to explore the question of landownership, how estates were managed, what improvements were made and to what extent the local landed families were affected by the growth of industry, there are a number of primary sources which you should consult. County Record Offices usually contain a large number of estate records and in order to discover who owned what land in the early nineteenth century you should consult the parish tithe map. The Tithe Commutation Act of 1836 resulted in accurate land surveys being made for most parishes in the country. A copy of the parish tithe map can usually be found at the local parish church and/or the local diocesan centre or Record Office. To evaluate land improvements in the eighteenth and early nineteenth centuries you should study local enclosure awards (again, usually found in the local Record Office). In fact, where the tithe map and enclosure award exists for a parish it is possible to construct a good picture of land use in this period. Another documentary source is the Board of Agriculture reports for the county. The Board of Agriculture was established in 1793 and almost its first undertaking was to publish a number of reports on the agriculture of the various counties of England. These reports usually deal with enclosures and other agricultural improvements.

One final word: those of you who are starting work on a project connected with your locality may well find W. G. Hoskins, *Local History in England* (Longman, 1972), an invaluable guide to sources and how to use them.

Addendum

Gillian Kay

Religion—ideas and organization—should not be thought a self-sufficient branch of history. It belongs in all three themes of the course, informing popular politics, and social policy official and unofficial. Yet the most plebeian congregations have to be viewed as local élites like more illustrious groups, as is shown by the 1851 Religious Census and Mayhew's revelations of theological ignorance in the slums.

The difficulty of studying religious history at local level is, of course, that (with exceptions) it was the well-known or middle-class Christians whose opinions and doings were recorded: they wrote in church journals and were reported in secular ones, their sermons were printed, their Lives and Letters piously published. With humbler people one relies more on local statistics plus the official transactions of churches. Many documentary collections are held by particular denominations and institutions. Miscellaneous materials, and parish records, can be found in local Record Offices; for an impression of the types of source, see the following, especially notes and bibliographies: Thompson, D. M., *Nonconformity in the Nineteenth Century* (1972); Inglis, K. S., *Churches and the Working Classes in Victorian England* (1963); Armstrong, A., *The Church of England, the Methodists and Society* (1973).

Poverty and Social Policy

This heading describes a branch of the occupations of governments and political élites; it also denotes a way of seeing most of the history of the period. Most matters of domestic politics, particularly from the 1790s, can be interpreted from this point of view, and manifest a huge range of attitudes to poverty and the poor. With this theme it is hard to separate the national from the local: history seems to be the history of ideas, and of actions, and of results. Josiah Sniggs, MP for the borough of Spinwich, writes pamphlets on the poverty and immorality of crossing-sweepers; the Sniggsites bring about a Royal Commission (evidence from Spinwich is submitted), then an Act controlling conditions in the sweeping industry. A student might research topics like 'Josiah Sniggs, Reformer'; 'Sniggs of Spinwich'—for which he would need *Hansard* and the proceedings of the Commission, as well as materials from the Spinwich Record Office, which might include poll-books, the local Archdeacon's Charges to his clergy, accounts of meetings in the local papers. With luck, the good evangelical Sniggs may have kept a diary, while his letters (in default of manuscripts) are doubtless reproduced in the official *Lives* of the recipients.

Or one might work on 'Spinwich and the operation of the Sweepers Act' (text of the Act; local papers; the local Record Office may have materials of the officers appointed to enforce the Act, etc.). For 'Spinwich in the 1840s: the Problem of Poverty', the Record Office may also have some of the Corporation's minutes and those of the various local bodies, centrally set up as authorities in local matters and proliferating in the mid-nineteenth century: notably for this purpose the Poor Law authorities. Among non-governmental social ventures, Spinwich possesses a utopian industrial estate, set up by a disciple of Robert Owen, with a mill and workers' houses and amenities surviving, and early plans and drawings. There are also several charitable foundations dating from the eighteenth century; and a National School, said by some to be a vehicle of social control for the Anglican establishment.

N.B. For centralized bodies you thus need more than the local sources; the Guardians' correspondence may be traceable locally, but for some purposes you also need the reports of the Poor Law Commissions. For a picture of kinds of source, see

Inglis, B., *Poverty and the Industrial Revolution* (1971)
Checkland, S. G., *The Rise of Industrial Society in England* (1964).
Kitson Clark, G., *An Expanding Society* (1967): see the chapter on 'The Modern State'.

Paper 3: Historical Field Studies and Industrial Archaeology

Ian Donnachie

1 Introduction: Historical Field Studies

The practising historian, whether amateur or professional, academic or research student, working in any branch of the discipline, must always have an intimate working knowledge of primary sources relevant to that particular field of study. You will, no doubt, be pretty familiar with the wide range of traditional primary source material available to the historian. It is the concern of this section to provide you with pointers to the scope for 'non-traditional' sources and their application to studies within the period 1750 to 1950. Stated in general terms these 'non-traditional' sources comprise the whole spectrum of physical heritage or 'history on the ground' associated with economic, technological, social and political change, including such fundamentals as (a) the changing social, economic and agricultural landscape, (b) agrarian and rural 'archaeology', (c) what is now widely and acceptably described as 'industrial archaeology'. We will be looking briefly at definitions of these three broad types of 'non-traditional' sources, but it is enough for the moment to cite a couple of practical examples. First, the historian investigating the economic and political interests of an eighteenth-century landed gentleman can derive a veritable wealth of information from historical field studies in the locality. He can follow up his documentary research with detailed studies of the landed estate, its farms and enclosures, its villages and housing, its transport and industries—all of which no doubt contribute in some measure to the social prestige and political influence of their owner. Second, and from much later in the period covered by this course, an investigation of early Local Authority housing, built in response to the Wheatley Act of 1924, would be all the more valuable if it included a detailed field survey of house-types and the various forms of accommodation provided.

Historians conscious of the value of field studies or 'non-traditional' primary sources must abandon (at least temporarily) their books for their boots. Analytical techniques are just as important in the field and generally field studies cannot be undertaken without preparatory work of a conventional character in documents or maps. It is likely that the follow-up to field research will also involve the use of the more traditional primary sources. It follows that all projects involving historical field studies will be of greater value if they integrate conventional research in written or printed sources. Another viewpoint would be to regard historical fieldwork of any kind as a useful complement to 'traditional' research in particular fields of history (and there are many conventional historians who would disagree with even this view), although field research might well stand on its own in certain contexts, especially where documentation is sparse or even non-existent.

The treatment of 'non-traditional' and physical sources in this section will be under the following headings:

(i)   Landscape and the Historian
(ii) Industrial Archaeology
(iii) History in the Countryside
(iv) Sources
(v)   Techniques of Field Recording

The last two sections will provide a work list of the wide range of traditional sources useful in such studies, as well as an indication of the possible scope for student research projects based primarily on fieldwork. The majority of these suggestions will relate to the three main themes of the course, though pointers to more general possibilities will also be given.

2   Landscape and the Historian

The growth of the disciplines of archaeology, historical geography and later of social and economic history has put increasing emphasis on the use of evidence provided by field studies and techniques. Archaeologists, by the very nature of their discipline, were the first to develop sophisticated field investigation, often a necessary aspect of research involving excavation. Victorian antiquarians were principally concerned with very basic—and often notoriously unscientific—historical field studies. Field investigation was given precision by later archaeologists, and it is probably fair to say that the current vogue for field research owes much to the natural emphasis given it by archaeology. Geographers also had an interest in the historical environment, in the evolution and history of landscape, and, above all, were concerned to stress the human impact on landscape over the centuries. Historical geographers, like H. C. Darby, editor of *An Historical Geography of England before 1800*, made outstanding contributions to their discipline and brought to the historical study of landscape the spatial techniques of the geographer. The historical geographer interests himself *inter alia* in man's imprint on the landscape, mainly in relation to land use, settlement, agriculture, industry and transport. It is understandable that he draws on a number of techniques from a wide range of disciplines, including not only geography but also history in all its branches, demography and geology, to name but three. Those interested in current methodology in historical geography will find

an excellent discussion of developments in Unit 14 of the D 281 course, *New Trends in Geography*.

The outstanding exponent of historical landscape studies in England is W. G. Hoskins, who, like Darby, marries the techniques of historian and geographer. In seeking to define such studies we cannot do better than quote from the preface of his outstanding pioneer work, *The Making of the English Landscape*:

[The geologist] explains to us the bones of the landscape, the fundamental structure that gives form and colour to the scene and produces a certain kind of topography ... but the flesh that covers the bones, and the details of the features, are the concern of the historian, whose task it is to show how man has clothed the geological skeleton during the comparatively recent past.

I am concerned with the ways in which men have cleared the natural woodlands; reclaimed marshland, fen and moor; created fields out of a wilderness; made lanes, roads, and footpaths; laid out towns, built villages; hamlets, farmhouses and cottages; created country houses and their parks; dug mines, and made canals and railways; in short, with everything that has altered the natural landscape.

Hoskins continues by saying that to discover much about the changing landscape 'we have to go to the documents that are the historian's raw material, and find out what happened to produce these results and when, and precisely how they came about'. Although documents are the historian's guide, the landscape itself 'is the richest historical record we possess', and when the two are combined 'the result is a new kind of history'.[1]

During the two hundred years which are the concern of this course the landscape of Britain altered dramatically. Between 1750 and 1950 many parts of Britain underwent a complete transformation and now-familiar elements were introduced into the landscape: mills, mines, factories, forges; roads, canals and railways; urban tenements and back-to-back housing, to cite several of the physical vestiges of the Industrial Revolution. Such has been the rate of change that districts which were almost wholly agrarian in the mid-eighteenth century are once more rural in character, though they wear the scars of nineteenth-century industrialization. In many a South Wales valley sheep graze on old coal tips or amidst the broken-down ruins of a once vibrant mining community.

The visual landscape of rural Britain was similarly transformed: over much of the country an Agrarian Revolution (as late as the 1840s in some more remote areas) created a landscape of enclosures, symmetrical field patterns, hedges, drains and ditches, woodlands and plantations, farmsteads, agrarian villages and country houses set in ornamental parks. The initiators of many of these changes were the landed élite—often as much concerned with economic development and political prestige as the merchants, entrepreneurs, mill and mine masters who created the industrial landscape which we have just touched upon.

So, essentially, historical landscape studies are concerned with the physical vestiges of past economic and social life. The historian with an interest in the evolving landscape since 1750 has at his disposal an immensely rich primary source for such topics as the following, loosely classified under the three main themes of the course:

British Elites
Economic interests of landowners
The landed estate
Planned villages
Enclosures and agrarian change
Country houses

Popular Politics
Pocket and Rotten Burghs
Mills, factories and Luddism
Enclosures and the 'Levelling Movement'
The countryside of 'Captain Swing', Riots
Highland Clearances

Poverty and Social Policy
Demographic Studies (i) migration
                    (ii) rural depopulation:
                        deserted villages
                 (iii) urbanization
Working and living conditions
Housing
Industrial and agrarian villages

These few examples serve to illustrate the scope for historical landscape studies as a complement to conventional research. We will move on now to look in more detail at the opportunities presented to the historian by industrial and rural archaeology.

3   Industrial Archaeology

Over the past decade or so one of the most exciting developments in the area of historical field studies has been the emergence of a new and immensely popular subject called (rather erroneously, as we shall see) by the hybrid name 'industrial archaeology'. A succession of writers and workers in this new field have attempted to define industrial archaeology, some taking a narrow view, others casting the net wider. An acceptable synthesis would be something like 'the study and recording of industrial and other remains, which illustrate the impact of changing technology on society', and as Dr Rodney Green, one of the early practitioners of industrial archaeology, has written, 'the methods of field study and record and even of excavation on appropriate sites make the subject properly a branch of archaeology, even though the results obtained are likely to prove of most value to the historian'.[2]

Although the majority of features which come under the heading of 'industrial archaeology' are of an essentially industrial character (such as old mills, factories, canals, etc.) the scope of the subject is such that a diversity of related physical features can legitimately be included. The historian applying the techniques of the industrial archaeologist in an examination of an old cotton mill community will necessarily look in detail at the adjoining workers' housing, the company store, school and church, as well as the factory itself. He will thus gain insights into living and working conditions—subjective impressions and objective data, which he could never obtain from documentary sources. Industrial archaeology thus provides the modern historian (and especially those interested in local history, or social and economic history) with the *réalité* of a physical heritage dating from the relatively recent past—a close parallel to the castles and ecclesiastical buildings which enthral the medievalist. The study of

industrial archaeology, then, has immediate relevance to a great deal of historical research in the post-1750 period.

The following list gives some idea of the range of features which interest the industrial archaeologist:

Agriculture and Rural Industry
Mills: water, wind, horse-driven
Farm buildings and machinery
Craftsmen's premises and workshops

Mining and Quarrying
Collieries
Stone quarries
Sand, gravel, chalk, clay pits
Iron mines
Salt mines, salt pans

Food Processing
Grain mills
Breweries
Distilleries

Metallurgy and Engineering
Iron and steel works
Blast furnaces
Engineering shops, foundries, forges
Shipyards

Textiles, Clothing, Leather
Wool, cotton and linen spinning mills
Handloom weavers' shop or cottages
Weaving mills
Tanneries

Chemicals, etc.
Chemical works
Gunpowder works
Brick and tile works
Cement works

Public Utilities
Gas: gas works
Electricity: electric power plant
Water supply and sewerage

Communications
Railways
Roads
Docks and harbours
Canals and inland navigation

Housing
Industrial housing: workers' housing of all kinds
Planned villages
Estate villages

Miscellaneous
Work houses
Poor houses
Gaols or bridewells

Of course, this is nothing like a complete list of industrial archaeology—merely a pointer to the sorts of details in the broader historical landscape of the eighteenth, nineteenth and early twentieth centuries, which are likely to prove worthy of investigation in your local area. In almost every research project involving industrial archaeology the historian will require to assess his sources in the ordinary way, examining their strengths, weaknesses and biases. At the same time, one cannot emphasize too strongly the importance of supportive documentary research, especially in relevant maps and secondary source material.

Undoubtedly the scope for industrial archaeology projects within the themes of this course is considerable. If you are contemplating such research do pay close attention to the later sections here which introduce you briefly to sources and field techniques, as well as suggesting possible projects and preparatory reading.

4 History in the Countryside

It would be wrong to suppose that the possibilities for research involving industrial archaeology are confined to the urban, industrial environment. In fact, all the evidence would seem to indicate that the scope is even greater in the countryside, as a glance at the publications in industrial archaeology up and down Britain reveals all too clearly. There are, of course, many 'arrested' industrial areas in the country, which during the past two hundred years supported mines and mills of all kinds, Cornwall and Wales being two pretty obvious examples which spring readily to mind. But, more significantly, just as industrial archaeology is a logical development of historical landscape studies in the industrial context, so what has been called 'rural archaeology' is a legitimate depth-study in the countryside. Rural archaeology could be defined as the study (*in situ* or in a museum, etc.) of the heritage associated with social, economic or political activity in the countryside. Examples include farm buildings, houses and machinery; estate villages and country houses; agricultural housing; abandoned villages or farmsteads; as well as a wide range of essentially rural crafts and industries (see for example, D 281 Unit 14, section 3).

It is undoubtedly difficult to draw a line between what is strictly 'industrial' or 'rural' in this context, particularly if we regard agriculture as an industry rather than a way of life; but it does seem important to stress the special nature of rural historical studies. In most parts of Britain the role of landowners in agricultural 'improvements', industrial or transport development and in the creation of planned communities was very significant, so that any project which has a rural setting is almost bound to touch on all these areas and probably range over the three course themes. This is especially true of research on local political personalities or popular politics, both themes being so closely related to the social and economic fabric of the countryside. Several of the examples cited in the section on *Landscape and the Historian* indicate clearly the inter-disciplinary nature of the research involved, and hint at the diverse sources the historian undertaking them would require to call into play.

5 Sources

Before the historian sets foot into the field on any project involving the examination of physical evidence, he must undertake a sensible amount of conventional research on documents or secondary sources. The aim of this section is to provide some indication of the types and range of material which could be consulted in a local borough or county Record Office and in the local collection of the

library. If you are in any doubt about historical sources you could usefully look at Arthur Marwick's *The Nature of History*, Chapter 5, or A100 Unit 6 on 'Primary Sources.'[3]

A Primary Sources

Documentary Records
The range of manuscript sources is wide. Here are a few examples which seem particularly relevant:
Local estate papers
Business and industrial records
Family papers (of landowners, politicians, businessmen)
Diaries and tours (good for topographical detail, local events, etc.)

Printed Records
Census returns
Parliamentary Papers

General Views of Agriculture (for English and Scottish counties)

Statistical Accounts (for Scottish Counties, published in the 1790s and 1840s)
Local Authority records (for public services, housing, Poor Law, etc.)
Newspapers

Maps and Plans
These are often central to any field research. The most useful maps are: medium-scale eighteenth and early nineteenth century maps (often of counties, containing a great wealth of detail); Ordnance Survey 6″ to 1 mile series (the earliest are most useful, dating from the 1830s and 1840s); larger scale plans (like the OS 25″ and private business or estate plans) and the wide variety of medium and large-scale OS maps of later nineteenth- and early twentieth-century date.[4]

Prints and Archive Photographs
Old prints and photographs are invaluable sources of information about buildings, such as housing and factories, and the social detail of old street scenes, etc.

B Secondary Sources

Again the range of possible source material is enormous and only a few relevant pointers can be given in the space available:

Victoria County Histories (For many English counties, including local parishes)
Statistical Accounts of Scotland (Third edition for many Scottish counties)

Local histories: a wide variety of city, borough, parish and regional histories
Company, business and industrial histories
Published records of such bodies as Friendly Societies and Trades Unions

C Oral Evidence

Oral evidence has its limitations, but it is obviously most valuable to have the memories or recollections of former workers in a mine or mill, or local inhabitants with a knowledge of past working and living conditions. The starting-points of most historical field research are likely to be secondary sources and modern maps followed by a survey of available documentation and map sources.

John Ainslie, The Stewartry of Kirkcudbright, *1797. A medium-scale map of a scale of about 1″ to 1 mile (roughly equivalent to a modern 1″ OS map). It shows a great amount of detail, including the estate, farms, mills, roads, etc. A good starting-point for a landscape or industrial archaeology survey.*

First edition of OS 6″ map, surveyed in mid-1840s. Much more detailed than map reproduced opposite. It gives a very clear picture of Gatehouse at the height of its prosperity as an industrial, estate and transport village in the mid-nineteenth century.

Depending on its nature, and depth of the field work, the documentary research is probably best done as a follow-up to findings. Such a project would thus have a sound basis in both conventional historical research and field study.

The following case-study in the use of sources gives some idea of the range of evidence available for a research project incorporating both general historical landscape studies and industrial archaeology, and which relates also to the three main themes of the course.

Gatehouse-of-Fleet: An Eighteenth-Century Estate Village

Gatehouse, in the Stewartry of Kirkcudbright, is a remarkable example of an eighteenth-century, planned estate village developed by a local landowner, James Murray of Broughton and Cally. Murray was in many ways the typical 'improving' landowner, interested in agriculture development, estate planning, industries and transport, as well as being heavily involved in local and national politics. The village of Gatehouse was developed after 1765, and laid out on the banks of the River Fleet to a symmetrical street plan, in the best traditions of Georgian town planning. By the mid-1780s, Gatehouse had a wide range of industries, including milling, brewing, tanning, foundries, and its most important activity, cotton spinning. It had a growing seaborne trade across the Solway Firth and was an important staging post on the Carlisle–Portpatrick turnpike. The Cally estate, on which Gatehouse stands. was also typical of many, having a fine mansion-house and ornamental parks, set in an increasingly prosperous, agrarian hinterland. Here, then, is an outstanding example of the opportunities presented to the historian by a landscape and community, which still preserves a great deal of its early nineteenth-century character. Not only is the history of this community and its founders extensively documented but much of the evidence of changes brought to the area by James Murray can still be seen on the ground. A selection of source material for this particular project is listed below, together with reproductions of maps, prints and other evidence relevant to a field study supported by documentary research.[5]

Plans

Greater detail on every aspect of the village community, its housing, industries and associated estate can be obtained from a wide range of plans in the estate and family archive, the Broughton and Cally Muniments, housed in the Scottish Record Office, Edinburgh. This is a very complete but nevertheless typical set of family records covering the period from the seventeenth to the present centuries.

Other Primary Sources

Broughton and Cally Muniments: the major archive source, mentioned above. Covers estate development, history of Gatehouse and its industries, public services and poor relief, local and national politics, family life.

Statistical Account of Scotland (Sir John Sinclair, ed.): parish accounts dating from 1790s. Similar series published in 1830s and 1840s is equally valuable.

Heron, R., *Observations Made in a Journey thro' the Western Counties of Scotland in the Autumn of 1792* (Perth 1799): immensely valuable contemporary account.

Old photographs and prints: a good example is reproduced here.

The Gatehouse cotton mills and part of the village by the river Fleet, from a print dated c. *1847 (Courtesy of Dr John Butt).*

Parish Registers

Parliamentary Papers: several Factory Inspectors visited Gatehouse in the course of their enquiries into working conditions in mills

Census Returns: useful demographic data after 1801, and especially so after 1841

6   Techniques of Field Recording

It must be obvious that the historian interested in the physical evidence of the past requires a wide range of talents but at the same time there is room for a variety of approaches. Enthusiasm coupled with a willingness to work in the fresh air on cold winter days are probably the best qualifications at the outset! Like other environmental study, historical field work requires a minimum amount of equipment before one can start. Assuming one has carried out the necessary preparatory research and has some clear idea of the questions one wishes to ask, fieldwork is likely to prove worth while, providing at least some of the answers and certainly raising new questions. If preparatory work is inadequate much of the effort which goes into any field exercise is likely to be useless.

First, a brief word about equipment. Listed below under (A) is really essential equipment, under (B) optional equipment for specialist fieldwork in aspects of industrial arehaeology, though probably also generally useful, and under (C) obvious personal accessories:

A   Clip-board
    Firm polythene cover
    Notebook
    Loose-leaf paper
    Graph paper (for simple measured drawings)
    Pen/pencil
    Ruler
    Rubber
    Camera

B   Steel tape (10-ft measure or metric equivalent)
    50-ft measure (or metric equivalent)
    Ranging rod

C   Solid footwear
    Warm and waterproof clothes (depending on weather, of course)
    Torch
    Rubber boots

Most of the things mentioned in list (C) may seem pretty obvious, and will be recognized as essential if exploring a dark and damp factory or mine (where obviously care must be taken). In addition, relevant maps are absolutely essential, the chosen map scales being appropriate to the breadth or depth of local research. A familiarity with the standard scale Ordnance Survey maps is almost a prerequisite for any fieldwork.

The current series is:

Small scale	1″ (Seventh Series) to 1 mile	
	2½″ to 1 mile	
Medium scale	6″ to 1 mile	
Large scale	25″ to 1 mile	

The 1″ series is suitable for a wide variety of general fieldwork, while the medium- and large-scale maps are appropriate for study involving such detail as field boundaries, streets and individual buildings. Certainly a valuable asset to any historical field study are photocopies of eighteenth- and nineteenth-century maps (like the examples reproduced on pp. 18–19), which allow immediate comparison of the modern landscape or existing physical evidence with past topography. Contemporary air photographs can also be useful, if readily available, because they often reveal detail not visible on the ground.

The major features of the historical landscape have already been described in Sections 2 and 4, and a detailed discussion of the constituent elements can be found in Chapters 6–9 of Hoskins's *Making of the English Landscape*. Although his principal concern is the landscape of Central and Southern England, the majority of his remarks are relevant to most of Britain (for Scotland, Ireland and Wales, see list of references at the end of this Unit). Clearly, general landscape studies within the three broad themes of the course are likely to incorporate documentary research and thus have much to commend them as a 'bridge' between the traditional approach and 'new' history.

Industrial archaeology does, however, require slightly specialized techniques. In a preliminary location survey the most important points to note are (a) the type of site (colliery, ironworks, workers' house, etc.) (b) its size, condition and construction, (c) its age (roughly), (d) its location (parish, town, street, grid reference, etc.) and (e) an estimate of its importance compared with other similar sites. The Council for British Archaeology (CBA) has produced a standard record card for industrial archaeological studies, an example of which is reproduced (*over*). Using these cards it is possible to build up a simple index of a particular group or type of sites. A separate card should be completed for each site, the information being transferred from a field notebook. In industrial archaeology, as in all aspects of historical investigation, negative evidence is important. The demolition or disappearance through decay of a site is worthy of record, as is the absence of typical features in a surviving site.

More detailed recording of such features as mill buildings or workers' housing will necessitate the use of camera and measuring tape. Simple measured drawings, diagrams and sketches are invaluable and add considerably to the value of the record. The main constructional or architectural details to note about any building are

(i) *Exterior:* overall dimensions (estimate), constructional materials (brick, stone, slate), number of storeys, number of windows in each storey (including attic dormers, etc.), type of windows (wood, cast-iron frame), type of roof (gabled, hipped, mansard, flat, etc.), chimneys (if any).

(ii) *Interior:* construction of vertical members (cast-iron, wood, concrete, steel girder, etc.), horizontal members, flooring (wood, tile), dimensions, thickness of walls, type (spiral, orthodox) and position of staircases, overall layout (doors, cupboards, fireplaces, etc., in dwellings).

Surveys of more specific industrial sites and remains like poor-houses, workers' housing, and even transport facilities, require an attention to detail which cannot be described here for lack of space. A number of works on in-

NATURE OF SITE (Factory,mine,etc.)			COUNTY	REF.No.
Grid Reference or Location	Industry	Dating	Parish/Township	Date of Report

DESCRIPTION: dimensions; present condition; architectural features etc.

(Further remarks or photo/sketch may be recorded on the back)
Machinery and Fittings

Danger of Demolition or Damage

Printed, Manuscript or Photographic Records

Reporter's name and address:-	Return to:-
Institution or Society:-	

C.B.A. Industrial Archaeology Report Card.

Standard record card for industrial archaeological studies, produced by the Council for British Archaeology.

dustrial archaeology can readily be consulted for detailed techniques of recording: the best are R. A. Buchanan's *Industrial Archaeology in Britain*, and J. P. M. Pannell's *Techniques of Industrial Archaeology*. A large number of regional and general studies in industrial archaeology are now available, and those appropriate to any local research project should certainly be consulted at an early stage.

7 Workers' Housing: Two Case-Studies

A potentially rich field of study within one of the course themes is workers' housing and related living and social conditions. The scope for local research on the history and industrial archaeology of working class housing from the Industrial Revolution onwards is well illustrated in the following case-studies. The first provides a summary of research work by Jeremy Lowe and his colleagues in the Welsh School of Architecture, of the University of Wales Institute of Science and Technology, Cardiff, on iron-workers' housing in South Wales, while the second summarizes a fieldwork project on agricultural cottages on the Dartington estates in South Devon, the result of research by a group of students under the leadership of Nathaniel Alcock.

(i) Standard Houses of the First Blaenavon Company: Housing in Blaenavon and Cwmavon

(from Lowe, J. B. and Anderson, D. N., *Iron Industry Housing Papers No. 4*, Welsh School of Architecture, UWIST, Cardiff, 1972)

This paper describes the standard houses built by the first Blaenavon Company during the period 1817–32. The ironworks were begun in 1789 and were successful in their early years, expanding rapidly during the Napo-

leonic Wars. A major reorganization of operations was carried out during 1817–19, and this work included the building of the first houses. Further batches of these houses were constructed up to the early 1830s.

The standard house was a single-fronted three-room dwelling two storeys high, usually laid out in long terraces of up to thirty units, but constructed in batches of five or ten (e.g. Upper New Rank, Blaenavon).

The main living-room was square, with a substantial brick-built fireplace. Behind this room, and leading off it, were a pantry and a small, unheated bedroom, roughly square in plan. Over the whole ground floor there extended a large unpartitioned sleeping chamber, open to the roof for its full height. The construction was as straightforward as the layout. The roof was covered with heavy Welsh slates laid in regular courses. They were carried on softwood rafters, which rested directly on the dividing walls of the houses. The whole interior shell of the house, including the underside of the slates, was lime-plastered and colour-washed, but there was no plastering either under the first floor or, originally, on the internal timber and brick-on-edge partitions. The stair was nearer to a ladder than a staircase, narrow and steep with shallow treads and no riser boards. It is said to have sloped backwards over the front door, climbing into an unprotected opening in the first floor; the openings could still be picked out in recently surviving houses, but there was no trace of the actual stairladder described by former residents.

The external construction was equally basic in character. The outside walls were of stone rubble and openings at ground-floor level were spanned by a single-brick arch with pronounced camber, backed inside by a rough timber lintel. The first-floor windows extended up to the main wall-plate. Originally there were either no window sills

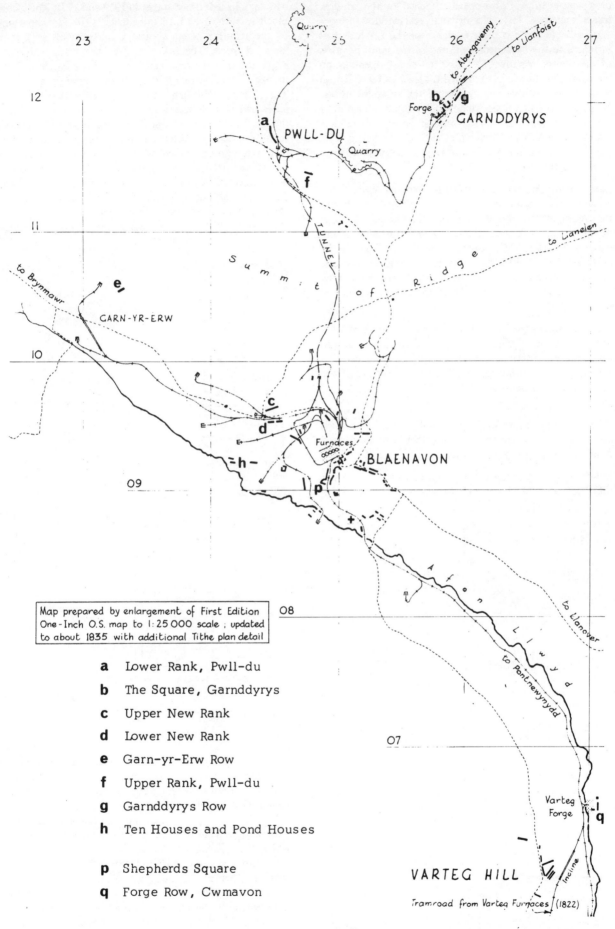

Map prepared by enlargement of First Edition
One-Inch O.S. map to 1:25 000 scale ; updated
to about 1835 with additional Tithe plan detail

a Lower Rank, Pwll-du

b The Square, Garnddyrys

c Upper New Rank

d Lower New Rank

e Garn-yr-Erw Row

f Upper Rank, Pwll-du

g Garnddyrys Row

h Ten Houses and Pond Houses

p Shepherds Square

q Forge Row, Cwmavon

*Location map of the standard houses of the First Blaenavon
Company*

or a simple timber drip-board attached to the window frame and now lost. No original rear-window frames survived, but there is clear evidence of the small arched openings to the back bedroom, and of the jamb position of the pantry window. The distribution of openings on the front elevation is both unique (at least as far as South Wales is concerned) and typical of the standard house. By placing the first-floor windows alternately above door and window openings to the ground floor, the builders could obtain an equal spacing at each floor level, despite the pairing of the houses. The arrangement gives a characteristic rhythm to the long façades.

Early sanitation was non-existent. Writing *circa* 1893, T. Dyne Steel recorded that around 1850 when he was in the employ of the second company, 'the sanitary arrangements of the workmen's cottages were deplorable. There was not a single W.C. convenience to the whole of the cottages of the works. On the matter being mooted one of the principal agents of the Company declared they were of no use and if constructed the people would not use them.'

The map shows the location of the eight groups of BCS houses known, or thought likely, to have been built to this pattern between 1817 and 1832. There were between 150 and 160 such houses in all, about one-third of the company's total housing stock in 1833.

The survey then describes the eight groups in turn, of which the following two present good examples. The descriptions are reproduced in edited form, together with associated drawings, maps and photographs.

Lower New Rank (letter (d) on map) formerly New Rank (SO 245 095), 20 houses in two separate blocks of 10,

BLAENAVON   LOWER NEW RANK

FRONT ELEVATION, as built.

FIRST FLOOR, in 1970 (left), as built (right)

GROUND FLOOR, in 1970 (left), as built (right)

CROSS-SECTION, as built

ELEVATION OF PARTITION (A)

was demolished in two stages in 1969 and 1971. The second block was surveyed in detail during 1970–71, when most of the features listed above in the general description were recorded. The numbering of the main wall-plates suggested that timbers were prepared for batches of five houses. There were at least three stages of alteration. The (1880) 1:2500 map shows that before that date sculleries had been added to the back of the houses. Nine of these sculleries were identical, built in large wedge-shaped refractory blocks intended for furnace construction; they were not provided with back doors. About 1908 the cross-partitions throughout the block were altered, a new door being opened in some houses by the fireplace. It was probably at this time that the stairs were moved. Further alterations took place after the Second World War. Both blocks can be seen on the (1827) 1″ OS map, somewhat indistinctly marked.

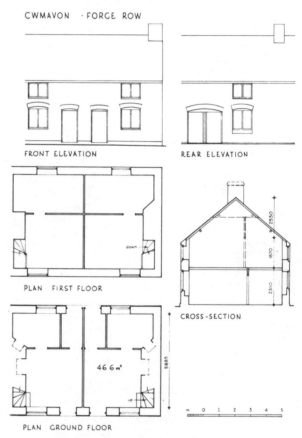

CWMAVON · FORGE ROW

FRONT ELEVATION   REAR ELEVATION

PLAN FIRST FLOOR   CROSS-SECTION

PLAN GROUND FLOOR

Forge Row, Cwmavon (SO 270 065), letter (q) on map is a terrace of 12 houses, in good condition and mostly still occupied. It stands on the steep hill-side above the main Pontypool road (A 4043), about 3 km south-east of Blaenavon. On the opposite side of the road, at a level well below the houses, is a small area of flat land beside the Afon Llwyd. This was the site of the Varteg Forge, from which the row takes its name; the forge was dismantled some time between 1845 and 1880. The history of this forge is obscure; it is not even certain which iron-works it was built to serve. It is not shown on the 1792 map of the Pontnewynydd Blaenavon tramroad but is clearly marked as 'Farteg Works' (Welsh 'F' equals English 'V') on the preliminary survey made in 1813 for the 1″ OS map. Forge Row itself is discernible on this map (despite its

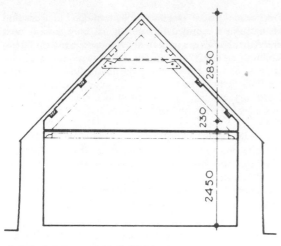

CROSS-SECTION

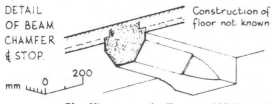

DETAIL
OF BEAM
CHAMFER
& STOP.

Construction of
floor not known

mm ⌊⌊⌊⌊⌊⌊ 0   200

Glyn View cottage (at Trosnant Old Furnace)

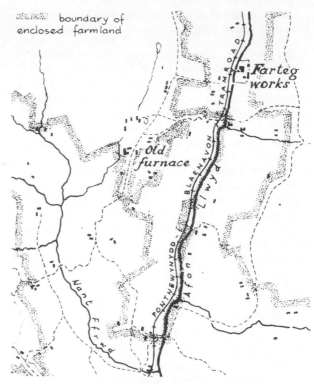

boundary of
enclosed farmland

*Simplified copy of part of 1813 preliminary survey for One-Inch
OS map. Scale approx. 1:31000.*

Forge Row, Cwmavon

Forge Row, Cwmavon, rear view

small scale), and there is evidence to suggest that it may date from before 1806.

Forge Row has a cross-section profile almost identical in proportion to that of the later BCS houses, but it is built to a four-room plan, the first floor being unequally divided. The windows on the back elevation appear to be original, suggesting that this partitioning of the sleeping chamber was always present. But it is difficult to see, while the houses remain occupied, how the present partition is connected to the original roof structure. However, whether Forge Row is regarded as a group of four-room or three-room houses, its detailed layout and construction are unique in the South Wales context. . . . Finally we must note the most uncommon feature of all for South Wales housing in the early 1800s. Forge Row is perhaps the only terrace of this date to have back doors, and it seems to have remained unique in this respect until the construction of the British Iron Works housing at Abersychan in 1825/26.

(ii) Rural Housing in Devon

(from Alcock, N. W. (ed.), *Dartington Houses: A Survey*, Exeter Industrial Archaeology Group/Dept. of Economic History, University of Exeter, 1972). In his introduction to this report (beautifully illustrated by drawings and layout plans), Nat Alcock writes:

The attraction of studying an old house includes the detective work to discover the original design and the stages of alteration, admiration for the craftsmanship of the builders, curiosity about just why it was built as we see it and perhaps above all the realisation that it embodies folk traditions and customs surviving from a vanished England. It has only recently been accepted that houses are important evidence of these traditions, of cultural patterns, agricultural techniques and economic conditions, and in Devon their systematic study has hardly begun. This is the more regrettable because the county has an extraordinary number and variety of old houses. A little is known of east Devon and of Dartmoor but nothing has been published from South Devon or the South Hams. In this survey, houses in Dartington parish have been examined. We have to concentrate on the detailed description of what was found, as the evidence for far-reaching conclusions has not yet been collected. However, one very important suggestion emerges, that there are distinctive differences between Dartington houses and those so far studied in other parts of the county.

There is no village of Dartington but the parish contains three or four hamlets and a number of isolated farms. New building of both nineteenth- and twentieth-century date has mostly taken place in the hamlets where it has rather obscured the original pattern but it is clear that they contained a number of small houses, possibly the cottages of landless labourers or of smallholders farming 5 to 15 acres.

The settlement patterns are outside the scope of this study and their unravelling would need careful consideration of all the available topographical evidence. Not one of the houses is likely to have been the first built upon its site and so the development of house names is not directly relevant here and is omitted.

The houses can be looked at from three aspects: (a) *plan* (b) *construction* (c) *decoration*; and (d) *outbuildings* need to be considered also.

On the following pages are two examples from the survey.

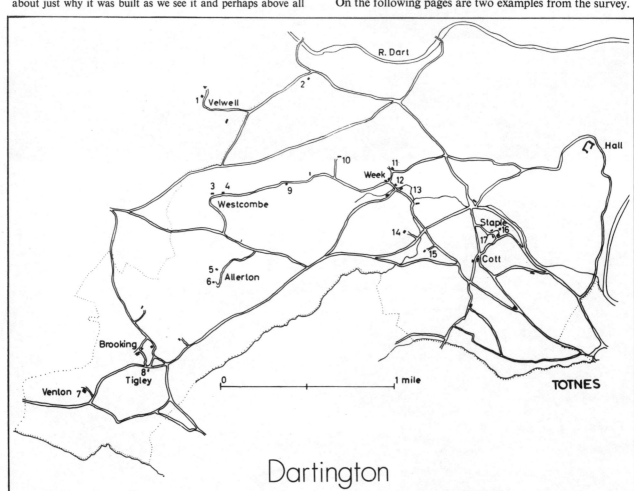

Map showing distribution of houses in Dartington.

Woodcott, Week

Site flat land in the valley bottom.

Materials rubble masonry, with a roof of grouted small local slates.

Plan three rooms roofed longitudinally; at the rear there is a large gable for the dairy (?) and a small gable for the stair, with a lean-to room beside this. The front wing is later.

Features there are straight masonry joints between the main range and all the other parts but the stonework is all of the same character. The front doorway (fig. 3) has a curved head. There are three stud-and-panel partitions but only one which is very plain is exposed. The hall beam' has a step stop and the door between hall and lean-to has a chamfered frame.

(Part of the house could not be examined in detail.)

Date and Development possibly there was a mid-sixteenth-century three-room house of which only the door survives as evidence of date. In the seventeenth century, a semi-circular stair and a dairy (?) were added at the rear, each with its own roof. The lean-to is perhaps a little later.

The hipped roof of the front wing suggests a late seventeenth- or eighteenth-century date for this addition.

Outbuildings all possibly eighteenth-century. There are a two-storey granary (A) and several small pyramidal roofed buildings (B, C), perhaps pigsties. The one across the road (C) may be a well-house. A number of identical small buildings exist in Week (fig. 20).

Example from Dartington Houses: A Survey, *showing field notes, layout plans and sketches.*

Lower Velwell

Example from Dartington Houses: A Survey, showing field notes, layout plans and sketches.

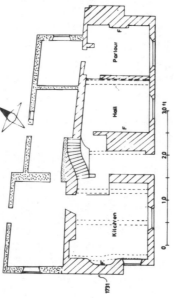

Site across a slight slope, facing south-east (and just in Rattery parish).

Materials rubble masonry. The roof was thatch until 1921 and is now slate.

Plan three-room with nineteenth-century additions at the rear.

Features there is a stud-and-panel partition between hall and parlour. The kitchen chimney has a 1731 date stone outside.

Roof some trusses have threaded purlins but there is much late replacement.

Date seventeenth-century from the few visable features. The entry was probably a cross-passage before it was blocked by the stairs.

Outbuildings there is a typical stable or shippon with granary over in rubble masonry (fig. 15) dated 1742.

8 Research Potential

This section gives an indication of the possible scope for student research projects based on a combination of field-work, industrial archaeology and traditional research. Each theme is followed by a brief note on approaches and possible source material. The starting-points for these and other projects should, of course, be the local Record Office or Library.

1 Factory and Working Conditions

This topic affords scope for a variety of approaches involving industrial archaeology and documentary research. Many types of factory/industry could be investigated, but whatever is chosen the project should aim to integrate physical evidence and documentation. Parliamentary Papers, and especially Reports of Factory Commissioners will prove invaluable.

Henriques, U. R. Q., *The Early Factory Acts and their Enforcement*, Historical Association, 1971.
Richards, J. M., *The Functional Tradition in Early Industrial Buildings*, Architectural Press, 1958; reprinted 1968.
Ward, J. T., *The Factory Movement 1830–1855*, Macmillan, 1962.

2 Economic and Social Interests of Landowners

The numerous possibilities of this theme include examinations of agricultural and estate development in the eighteenth and nineteenth century, industrial interests (mills, factories, mines, etc.), transport, (canals, ports and harbours, railways) and housing. The best sources are family and estate records, which are also immensely valuable for the more general interests of landowners, e.g. national and local government.

Ward, J. T. and Wilson, R. W. (eds.) *Land and Industry: The Landed Estate in the Industrial Revolution*, David & Charles, 1971.

3 Working-Class Housing

There are many possibilities in this topic, depending primarily on location. Five main types of workers' housing are likely to be of interest:

 (i) company or estate villages (including factory, colliery and agricultural housing)
 (ii) urban back-to-back housing (throughout much of industrial England and Wales)
 (iii) tenement housing (an essentially Scottish feature)
 (iv) workers' cooperative housing
 (v) early Local Authority housing (mostly late 1920–30s)

This sort of project can either be based primarily on field research or combine field survey with documentary work. The obvious sources are estate, company or Local Authority records.

Chapman, S. D. (ed.), *The History of Working-class Housing*, David & Charles, 1971.
Orwell, G., *The Road to Wigan Pier*, Penguin, 1962.
Parker, V., *The English House in the Nineteenth Century*, Historical Association, 1970.
Roberts, R., *The Classic Slum. Salford Life in the First Quarter of the Century*, Manchester University Press, 1971.
Tann, J., *Working-class Housing in Nineteenth-century Britain*, Lund Humphries, 1971.

Tenement housing development at New Lanark.

4 Poor Houses and Workhouses

Although the workhouse was a feature of pre-nineteenth century poor relief, the majority surviving in one form or another today (mostly as institutions or hospitals) date from the years after the New Poor Law of 1834. There are opportunities for research involving surveys of surviving institutions, integrating documentary research on Poor Law and relevant Local Authority records.

5 Sanitation and Water Supply

This is a similar project to (4), involving investigation of public utilities in the nineteenth- and early twentieth-century contexts, also making use of Local Authority archives and Parliamentary Papers.

Chadwick, E., *Report on the Sanitary Condition of the Labouring Population*, 1842, new ed. (with introduction by M. W. Flinn), Edinburgh University Press, 1965.
Flinn, M. W., *Public Health Reform in Britain*, Macmillan, 1968.

6 Case Studies of 'Captain Swing' Riots

Projects arising from this suggestion would essentially be concerned with reassessments of local agrarian agitations involving mobbing, threshing-machine breaking and rick burning in central and southern England. Research would seek to combine documentary and field evidence, e.g. a field and photographic survey of farms involved in local 'Captain Swing' outbreaks. Essential reading for anyone attracted by this project is:

Hobsbawm, E. J. and Rudé, G., *Captain Swing*, Lawrence & Wishart, 1969.

7 Local Luddism

A parallel project in the industrial environment, linking factory localities or surviving remains with Luddite outbreaks, and using documentation available at a local Record Office or Library.

Thomis, M. I. *The Luddites: Machine Breaking in Regency England*, David & Charles, 1971.

8 Chartist Land Company Estates

The Chartist Land Plan produced many agrarian experiments in central and southern England which have left much to interest the historian both on the ground, and in documents. There is clearly scope for projects involving an examination of local Chartist land settlements.

Hadfield, A. M., *The Chartist Land Company*, David & Charles, 1970.

9 The Environment of Radical Agitations or Popular Protest

The idea behind these projects, like those on 'Captain Swing' or Luddite riots, would be to go over the ground of a local Radical agitation, etc., describing the physical as well as the documentary evidence. The result could be an interesting reconstruction of events at the time—a sort of historical photo-journalism.

Notes

1 Hoskins, W. G., *The Making of the English Landscape*, Hodder & Stoughton, 1955.
2 Green, E. R. R., *The Industrial Archaeology of County Down*, HMSO, 1963.
3 The best guides to local sources in England are: Stephens, W. B. *Sources for English Local History*, Manchester University Press, 1973, and Rogers, A. *This Was Their World: Approaches to Local History*, BBC Publications, 1972.
4 Two useful guides to OS maps for the historian are J. B. Harley's *The Historian's Guide to Ordnance Survey Maps*, National Council of Social Service, 1964, and his *Maps for the Local Historian: A Guide to British Sources*, also NCSS, 1972.
5 For a comprehensive list of primary and secondary sources see my *Industrial Archaeology of Galloway*, David & Charles, 1971.

References

Beresford, M., *History on the Ground: Six Studies in Maps and Landscapes*, Methuen, 1957 (rev. ed. 1971).
Buchanan, R. A., *Industrial Archaeology in Britain*, Penguin, 1972.
Corfe, T., *History in the Field*, Blond Educational, 1970.
Darby, H. C., *An Historical Geography of England Before A.D. 1800*, Cambridge University Press, 1951.
Donnachie, I., 'The Classification of Industrial Monuments', *Industrial Archaeology*, vol. 6, no. 1, 1969.
Donnachie, I., *The Industrial Archaeology of Galloway*, David & Charles, 1971.
Emmison, F. G., *Archives and Local History*, Methuen, 1966.
Finberg, H. P. R. and Skipp, V. H. T., *Local History: Objective and Pursuit*, David & Charles, 1967.
Green, E. R. R., *The Industrial Archaeology of County Down*, HMSO, 1963.
Hoskins, W. G., *The Making of the English Landscape*, Hodder & Stoughton, 1955.
Hoskins, W. G., *Local History in England*, Longmans, 1959.
Hoskins, W. G., *Fieldwork in Local History*, Faber, 1967.
Mills, D. (ed.), *English Rural Communities: the Impact of a Specialised Economy*, Macmillan, 1973.
Pannell, J. P. M., *Techniques of Industrial Archaeology*, David & Charles, 1966.
Raistrick, A., *Industrial Archaeology: An Historical Survey*, Eyre Methuen, 1972.
Rogers, A., *This Was Their World: Approaches to Local History*, BBC Publications, 1972.
Stephens, W. B., *Sources for English Local History*, Manchester University Press, 1973.

Paper 4: The Mid-Nineteenth Century: Relevant Source Material

Christopher Harvie

Introduction

The main purpose of these papers has been to assist you in choosing a topic for research. My intention in this section is to concentrate on material, for the most part readily available, which was produced in, and is therefore particularly useful for the study of, the Victorian period. I am going to deal with material which 'bridges' local history and the national context in which our themes have significance. Clive Emsley, Anthony Coulson and John Golby elsewhere refer to the sort of records available in public collections at national, county or borough level. In the nineteenth century such information becomes both more plentiful, more systematic, and more readily available in printed form; the industrial revolution was, after all, a revolution in communications as well. The railway, the telegraph and later the telephone, the penny post, the mass-circulation newspaper, the typewriter—any one of this random selection had a dramatic effect not only on the society it served but on the information we now have available on it. The expansion in the technology of print probably meant that the latter half of the nineteenth century was the most extensively *recorded* epoch in history (the subsequent development of verbal and visual means of communication—telephone, radio, television—has greatly reduced this).

This vast amount of information had to be controlled, publicized and made accessible, but it also enabled the creation of great uniform systems of information storage. Without them industrial society could not have survived, and since they were important, they remain reasonably accessible. It is with such material, much of which can be found in your county library, that I want to deal.

What follows are notes on the historical evidence available in such 'long-run' sources, and hints on how to consult and interpret it. Where some orthodox sources were affected by nineteenth-century developments I have mentioned this as well, although others (like *Hansard* or Parliamentary Papers) are catered for in other parts of the Introduction.

Historians and Victorians

I have based this section on a diagrammatic representation (*above right*) of the bibliography of D. A. Hamer's *Liberal Politics in the Age of Gladstone and Rosebery* (Oxford, 1972)—a book typical of recent detailed research into Victorian politics. The diagram shows the dates of publication of the 'secondary' works Hamer cites. These are the sort of works you will find useful as 'hyphens' to connect research done at a local level with a general overview of nineteenth-century history. This sort of overview is necessary if you are to see your own work in proportion to your chosen theme in its historical period. The work of professional historians formulating theories of economic, social and political development provides at least a model of such relationships, to be tested and if necessary discarded. To ignore their work is to risk being over-specialized, antiquarian and possibly irrelevant.

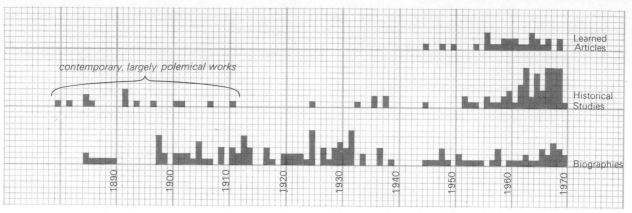

Dates of works cited in D. A. Hamer, Liberal Politics in the Age of Gladstone and Rosebery.

However, as the diagram indicates, there are problems: the serious study of Victorian history is relatively recent, although the recovery of the reputation of the period from the arty 'debunking' of Lytton Strachey and his ilk dates from the 1930s, when G. M. Young edited the symposium *Early Victorian England* (Oxford, 1934) and distilled from it his own brilliant essay *The Portrait of an Age* (Oxford, 1936), and George Kitson Clark's work on Sir Robert Peel (*Peel and the Conservative Party*, Bell, 1929). Kitson Clark's role as research supervisor at Cambridge produced a notable group of historians, now broadcast throughout Britain and America. Both Young and Kitson Clark (though by no means all their followers) were politically active Conservatives, and in due time their work was bound to produce a radical reaction. This effectively came after 1956, when the destruction of orthodox Communism's hold on British left-wing historians meant the regeneration of radical critiques of nineteenth-century society, based on Marx but not shackled to the traditional exposition of his thoughts by the Communist Party. E. P. Thompson's *The Making of the English Working Class* is the most impressive product of this new wave to date, and it is significant that he ends his preface with a hostile reworking of a passage from Kitson Clark's *The Making of Victorian England* (Methuen, 1962). Thompson speaks of his desire to 'rescue the poor stockinger, the "obsolete" hand-loom weaver, the "utopian" artisan, and even the deluded follower of Joanna Southcott, from the monstrous condescension of posterity', mirroring a sentence of Kitson Clark's in which he writes of rescuing the Victorian middle classes from 'the ignorance of posterity'. The interest in labour and working-class history has continued to have a connection with the contemporary development of the radical left in Britain, and this has influenced some controversies, notably that on the passing of the Second Reform Bill in 1867 (where the Tory historian Maurice Cowling discovers, in *1867: Disraeli, Gladstone and Revolution* (Cambridge, 1968), a 'Labour school of history'—comprising Thompson, Eric Hobsbawm and Royden Harrison) and in the study of the development of Victorian administration, where Jenifer Hart (in *Past and Present*, No. XXXI, 1965) identifies a 'Tory school of history' including Kitson Clark, the late W. L. Burn, Oliver MacDonagh, David Roberts and Royston Lambert.

It would be fair to say, though, that since the late 1950s the initiative has passed to the 'straight-line professionals'

as Arthur Marwick has called them. Present-day British historical studies are—as they have never been before—centred on the nineteenth century. In the *ASLIB Index to Theses*, those with nineteenth-century concerns make up the largest single group, 21 out of 54 in 1969 compared with 12 out of 51 in 1950. If we take into account the growing involvement of American historians—exemplified by the founding of the interdisciplinary quarterly *Victorian Studies* at the University of Indiana in 1957—this predominance is accentuated.

This rise in 'input' has resulted in a considerable growth in the 1960s in the number of scholarly secondary works—as shown in the diagram—with a parallel growth in learned articles. However, there is one serious drawback which affects their availability (and consequently the use you will be able to make of them). Written for a university market (of teachers rather than students) such works are both expensive and difficult to purchase. A hardback of the 'scholarly monograph' type can now cost up to £7, and paperback reprints are rare. Moreover, they are unlikely to be stocked by any but the largest libraries. In due course the findings of such research may penetrate to the level at which they are readily (and cheaply) available to students in the shape of 'works of historical synthesis', but this involves a time-lag which, in this rapidly developing discipline, can obscure the advances that are being made.

Biography

For the 'set book' of this part of the course I have chosen Robert Blake's *Disraeli* (Methuen, 1966), not only because it is an important treatment of two of our main themes (British Élites and Popular Politics) but also because it is representative of a major type of historical source which, though admittedly variable in quality, is on the whole widely available both as a primary and a secondary source. (This too you can see from the diagram—notice the 'spread' of biographies from the later nineteenth century on. Even where the stream of 'straight' historical writing appears to dry up, they continue to emerge.) It's worth while enquiring why this should be and how useful this source is.

The art of biography, in its modern sense, dates more or less from the eighteenth century, in particular from James Boswell's *The Life of Samuel Johnson LL.D.* (1791).

That extraordinary work has never been equalled as a portrait, but it had an enduring effect in introducing a new standard of rigour. Boswell wrote, in his first chapter, defining his principles:

Wherever narrative is necessary to explain, connect, and supply, I furnish it to the best of my abilities; but in the chronological series of Johnson's life, which I trace as distinctly as I can, year by year, I produce, wherever it is in my power, his own minutes, letters or conversation, being convinced that this mode is more lively, and will make my readers better acquainted with him, than ever most of those were who actually knew him, but could know him only partially; whereas there is here an accumulation of intelligence from various points, by which his character is more fully understood and illustrated.

This contrasted with previous practice—including that of Johnson—which used the *Life* as a sort of human peg on which to hang the author's own opinions, either favourable or condemnatory, and not necessarily about the person himself, but with questions of politics, religion or cultivated taste. Henceforth most, though not all, biographies tended to be comprised for the most part of primary sources created by, or about, the subject himself. Disraeli himself was a notable exception; his family *Memoir* (1858) was partly myth, his *Life of Lord George Bentinck* political propaganda (Blake, pp. 3–10, 264). Nonetheless, during the nineteenth century, biography became a major literary industry, culminating in the mammoth project of the *Dictionary of National Biography*.

Political biography came to take three main forms. Firstly, there were what would now be called 'campaign biographies' of political personalities, issued during the lifetime of their subjects with the purpose of 'selling' them to the electorate (or alternatively, of 'knocking' them). You will find two such referred to by Blake on p. 350. Along with this could be classed autobiographical works, where a particular politician thought fit to explain his policy in terms of his own career. Gladstone alone in the nineteenth century was given to this; it is on the whole a twentieth-century phenomenon. Every prime minister since Balfour who has not actually died in office or shortly afterwards (except Stanley Baldwin and Sir Alec Douglas-Home), has favoured the public with his memoirs. These are usually very lengthy and very uninformative.

The next type, which followed strictly in the tradition of Boswell, was the heavyweight 'official' biography. 'Official' can usually be taken to mean that the biographer has had unrestricted access to the papers of the personality concerned; it usually follows his death by a decade or so, and such works tend to be written by a close political colleague, a member of his family, or a journalist on a party newspaper. Gladstone's was written by his devoted acolyte John Morley (1903), Salisbury's by his niece Lady Gwendolen Cecil (1921–32) and Campbell-Bannerman's by J. A. Spender, the editor of the Liberal *Westminster Gazette* (1923).

The 'official' biography tended either to subsume, or to drag in its wake, various memoirs by individuals who had known, supported, or opposed the subject concerned. The quality of these is infinitely variable; some, like James Bryce's essay on Disraeli in *Studies in Contemporary Biography* (1905), have been acclaimed as first-rate analyses of individuals (by Norman Gash in *The Historical Journal*,

1968), others are mere anecdotage or rehashes of material already published.

Finally there is what I would call the 'historical retrospective' type of biography. As you can see from the diagram, the growth in this sort of writing has mirrored the growth in the writing of historical monographs. However, the parallel is not exact. Biography is not, as Blake implies in his treatment of Peel's fall in Chapter X, totally at one with the history of the subject's times. The subject's own behaviour has pride of place, and so anything written about specific individuals—Queen Victoria, Winston Churchill—will always have an attraction for the general reader: and the attraction extends to writers who are not professional historians but politicians (like Mr Roy Jenkins) or private individuals who simply have an interest in, or affinity with, a specific individual or simply write biographies for a living. As biography isn't straight history, affinity and sympathy with one's subject are important. However, the fact that a biographer is not 'plugged into' the concerns of professional historians dealing with his subject's period can result in the biography failing to answer certain of the critical questions historians would wish to pose about the subject's role in important political developments, which are only of oblique interest to the biographer.

Each type of biography has its own advantages and disadvantages as a historical source. The 'campaign biography' tells us what impression an active politician wanted to make on his supporters or opponents. The autobiography gives some idea of his own responses and attitudes of mind. The 'official' biography usually gives a wide range of contemporary primary sources (although this can be affected by the discretion a biographer has to have in alluding to persons still living). At the very least all of these flesh out the figures in political controversies, creating personalities who can be motivated by pressures other than the specifically political. Gladstone with his High-Churchmanship, his embarrassingly wide range of intellectual interests, memorializing his colleagues with questions about Homer: Disraeli with his con-man past, his debts and mistresses, his novels, his Semitism: they are otherwise two-dimensional, and to that extent unreal.

Biographical Series

The classic achievement of Victorian biography was the *Dictionary of National Biography*, planned by the publisher George Smith and the literary critic and philosopher Leslie Stephen, in 1882. The first volume *Abbadie-Anne* was issued in January 1885, and by 1901 the original project was completed. This included notices of prominent national figures who died before 1901; personalities dying after 1886 whose names came early in the alphabet were tidied into the 'First Supplement' which concluded the original project. Subsequently, supplements have been issued for 1901–11, 1912–21, 1922–31, 1932–41, 1942–51 and 1952–61. Coverage within the volumes is alphabetical (as in the original editions) but you have to know the decade in which your subject died. You can find this out by consulting the cumulative index, 1901–61, in the most recent volume.

Writers in the original series are indicated by initials: i.e. L. S. = Leslie Stephen; there is a key in volume I.

Since 1922 contributors' names have been given in full.

The *D.N.B.* is particularly valuable for national political, military, religious, artistic and literary élites; it is weak on industrialists and working-class leaders. Naturally its standards of scholarship (especially on pre-nineteenth-century Britain) have subsequently been superseded, but it remains the most important single source of biographical information on Victorian Britain. You will find it particularly useful to 'establish the credentials' of contemporary authorities—it is useful to know, for instance, that P. W. Clayden's *England under Lord Beaconsfield* (1880) was written by a radical nonconformist journalist on the Liberal *Daily News* (see *D.N.B.* 2nd supplement, 1901–11, p. 370); we can accordingly expect more Liberal propaganda than objective scholarship. It is also a helpful bibliographical source.

The *D.N.B.* had some pretensions to literary style, and it knew its place in the pecking order of upper-class Britain. The unexceptional talents of Edward VII got 64 pages in the second supplement while Karl Marx and Friedrich Engels were ignored (not on the grounds that they were German, as many exiles qualified). A more comprehensive, though less literary treatment was provided by Frederic Boase's *Modern English Biography* (6 vols. 1892–1921) which has 30,000 entries covering personalities who died between 1851 and 1900. Like the *D.N.B.* it can be found in most larger libraries. It is alphabetically arranged, but the last three volumes are supplements to the first three, covering deaths between 1890–1900 but also containing additional names from the earlier period. So you will find that you will frequently have to look in two places for an entry. Information is highly abbreviated and condensed, but bibliographical details are given. For information on personalities dying after 1897 *Who Was Who* can be consulted, though this is based on 'autobiographical' data and so can be misleading. Moreover, it's as socially unbalanced as the *D.N.B.* In fact we have no biographical source dealing with those who died in the twentieth century as comprehensive as Boase.

On the whole, as we can expect, the established classes are better served, through registers of schools, universities, regiments, professional organizations, *Burke's Peerage and Landed Gentry*, etc. (admittedly of variable quality) than anyone else. It is only quite recently that attempts have been made to remedy this, like the current *Dictionary of Labour Biography*, edited by John Saville and Joyce Bellamy, and Brian Harrison's *Dictionary of British Temperance Biography* (Labour History Society, 1973).

Encyclopaedia and Dictionaries

The Victorian desire for systematized information was exemplified by elaborate reference works like the *Dictionary of National Biography*. Along with this must be classed the *Encyclopaedia Britannica* and the *Oxford English Dictionary*. The eleventh edition of the *Encyclopaedia*, published in 1911 and largely written by British academics, drew substantially on the research generated by the other two works and is, at the very least, an invaluable bibliographical guide. Moreover, being written for active public men, rather than the 'status-conscious' household consumer (as with subsequent editions) it attempted to convey an accurate account of how processes

and institutions functioned. For instance the article on the *Poor Law* is seven pages long and gives a very useful abstract of the 1834 act. The *Oxford English Dictionary*, projected in 1881 and printed between 1886 and 1921, is essentially a massive historical source. It was planned on historical lines, defining the meanings of words through their past usage; i.e. if we looked up 'élite' in the *O.E.D.* we would find:

Élite (eli·t) sb³ [F. *elite* (in O.Fr. *eslite, elite*: see prec.) selection, choice; in mod. use *concr.* that which is chosen: med. L. *ēlecta* choice, f.L. *ēligĕre*: see ELECT *v.*] The choice part or flower (of society, or of any body or class of persons). 1823 Byron *Juan* XIII.LXXX, With other Countesses of Blank—but rank; At once the 'lie' and the élite of crowds. 1848 W. H. Kelly tr. *L. Blanc's Hist. (of) Ten Y(ears).* i. 439. The élite of the Russian nobility. 1880 GOLDW(IN) SMITH in Atl(antic) Monthly No. 268: If we take into consideration . . . the élite of a comparatively civilised generation.

When you have to provide definitions of words with a precise political significance in the nineteenth century—often quite different from their contemporary meaning—you will find the *O.E.D.* a very useful source.

Gazetteers, Guides, Directories

A nation whose economy depended increasingly on the integration provided by improved transport required convenient works of geographical reference. For that reason these remain, even today, accessible to the general reader, and frequently they yield considerable information on both urban and rural society. The six-volume *Ordnance Gazetteer of Scotland* (1896) has, in Volume III, an eighty-page article on Glasgow, with a couple of good maps, which gives details of population, industries, topography, municipal government, architecture and so on; in fact, one of the best accounts of the late nineteenth-century city that can be found. A *Gazetteer* exists in the same format for England and Wales, but is less comprehensive in scope. This is mainly due to the fact that, in the 1790s and the 1830s, Scottish society was surveyed in great detail through the *First* and *New Statistical Accounts*. These were compiled by parish ministers against a questionnaire formulated by the agricultural improver, Sir John Sinclair of Ulbster, which surveyed each parish under five main heads:

(i)   Topography and Natural History
(ii) Civil History
(iii) Population
(iv) Industry
(v)   Parochial Economy

These accounts could be anything from ten to sixty pages long, and averaged about twenty-five (save of course in the case of the cities). Their detailed and systematic descriptions act as a kind of standard for other accounts. With few exceptions this standard was not maintained in England. A scheme of Sinclair's for a *Statistical Account* was vetoed by the church authorities, although the publications of his 'Board of Agriculture' (a private, not a government, body) entitled *A General View of the Agriculture of Derbyshire*, etc., provide a large amount of systematic information about industry as well as agriculture for the earlier part of the century.

Absence of such surveys, thoroughly grounded in the social science techniques of the time, was reflected in the career of the ambitious *Victoria History of the Counties of England* (1899–). Although the general introductions to the country volumes tended to have some treatment of the general development of population, agriculture and industry, this was subordinate to the antiquarianism of the 'hundred' surveys which followed.

The hand of the antiquarian fell heavily even over the industrial town; with reason, as the face of such towns was changing and expanding, upsetting permanently the arte-facts of a previous society. Nonetheless, the creation of an industrial society itself remains obscure in many parts of the country, and ascertainable only through primary evidence, like maps, local authority records and, where they exist, company papers. Some industrial towns pro-duced local guide/histories, usually of a fulsomely lauda-tory kind, for instance the *Illustrated Guide to Sheffield* by Pawson and Brailsford published in 1862, which at least gives a good account of the city and its industries from the manufacturer's point of view. But the staple printed source must be the *Directories* printed by private firms like Kelly & Co. which indicate at least who the controlling groups in a town were likely to be. These are, to this extent, an élite source; what they do not convey about the social life of the mass of the population can be gauged by contrasting them with private surveys like Seebohm Rowntree's *Poverty: A Study of Town Life* (1902), which deals with working-class life in York.

The Newspaper Press

This was a period of growth and change for newspapers. Provincial weeklies had existed since the eighteenth century but there were no provincial dailies in 1846. By 1880 there were 121, and the position of *The Times* as the sole mass (60,000+) circulation newspaper had been overtaken by the *Daily News* (1846–1930) and the *Daily Telegraph* (1855–).

Although the newspapers are an important source, they can also be a difficult one to consult. It's worth bearing a few simple points in mind: first of all, the value of *The Times*.

Relatively few newspapers are indexed. *The Times* is, and its index is widely available. Probably your county library has a copy, even if it doesn't have the paper itself. Besides giving a direct reference (by date, page and column) to people and events, it is also useful as a means of finding out just when person X or event Y first 'came into the news'; and thereafter, just how newsworthy they were. Then, *The Times* was almost semi-official, and published *in their entirety* parliamentary debates, politicians' public speeches, and the more important court cases. What's more, most provincial newspapers took their national news re-ports verbatim from *The Times*, which means that you can, on the whole, expect that what *The Times* reported would be the basis of, say, the *Oxford Chronicle*'s coverage of national issues. (At least until about the 1880s, when local papers gave up carrying national news, or, if they were dailies, depended on news agency cables.)

Most towns had more than one weekly paper. Such papers were usually of opposed political views, so it's worth

while checking up on what their politics in fact were in the *Newspaper Press Directory*, published annually from the 1850s on.

Periodicals

The Victorian age was the great age of the quarterly, monthly or weekly review. 'Review' in fact describes what most of these publications were, as they consisted substan-tially, sometimes entirely, of critical articles. So they are, at the very least, a means of surveying in abbreviated form many books which played an important role in Victorian society. (It is probable, for instance, that far more of the 'educated classes' gained an idea of what Darwin was about in 1859 by reading articles on him in reviews than by reading *The Origin of Species*.)

One point you have to bear in mind, however, is political bias. Right from the beginning, with the publication of the Whig *Edinburgh Review* in 1802, the reviews adhered strongly to political parties, and this tended to influence strongly the 'line' their contributors took. (See Webb, p. 181.) This begins to decline somewhat in importance by the middle of the century, when the personnel of the reviews changes, from politicians like Brougham and Francis Jeffrey, who were concerned to put over a party view, to 'men of letters'—usually young university Fel-lows who, because of the clerical domination of Oxford and Cambridge, could not get teaching jobs in the universities themselves. These men, like John Morley, editor of *The Fortnightly* (1865–1954) and Leslie Stephen, editor of *The Cornhill*, tended, because of their 'alienation' from established society to become politically radical. The most extreme development of this tendency was provided by the Positivists (believers in the 'religion of society' of Auguste Comte) who in the 1860s embraced the cause of the trade unions.[1] In this way even such an 'élitist' source can convey to us a fair amount of information about popular politics.

Illustrated Periodicals

The illustrated weekly or monthly started in Britain about 1832, and has traditionally provided a good range of graphic source material for the historian. The engrav-ings from the *Illustrated London News* (1842–), *The Graphic* (1869–1932) and cartoons from *Punch* (1840–) and *Vanity Fair* (1868–1929) have been frequently quarried. However, these have certain limitations: social reportage in the *Illustrated London News* was conditioned by the predelictions of the middle classes who subscribed to it. So the working classes tended to be featured only as the victims of disasters or the instigators of particularly serious strikes and riots, or as a 'background' to the unveiling of some new piece of industrial equipment. And all of this could pale into total irrelevance if there was competition from a foreign war or a royal marriage.

Punch began similarly as a radical observer of British society and some of its cartoonists, Charles Leech, Dicky Doyle and George Cruikshank, stood in the tradition of Hogarth and Gillray. But after about 1850, when it was

1 See Royden Harrison, *Before the Socialists* (Routledge, 1965)

sold to its printers, Bradbury and Evans, it became more conservative and is only really useful as a commentary—on the whole a conservative one—on parliamentary politics through Sir Henry Lucy's reports and the cartoons of Tenniel, Sambourne, Furniss and Tennyson Reed. If you know a lot about the parliamentary politics of the time, you can even find them funny.

Surveys and Year Books

Government enquiries were increasingly supplemented by the activities of private bodies or abbreviated in the publications of commercial concerns. The annual conference reports of bodies like the *British Association for the Advancement of Science* (1831–) and the *National Association for the Promotion of Social Science* (1857–86) are a valuable mine of information. The *British Association* conferences were peripatetic, and bear on the social problems of the areas they visited. In the twentieth century it has prepared 'scientific surveys' of such areas which contain much historical and statistical information, e.g. *A Scientific Survey of South-Eastern Scotland* prepared for the Edinburgh conference of 1951. Local philosophical, scientific and statistical bodies also printed journals along the same lines.

On the other hand, commercial concerns produced abbreviated versions of government statistics, policies and personnel in yearbooks. Tne *Annual Register* dates from the eighteenth-century, *Whitaker's Almanac* and *The Statesman's Year Book* from the 1860s. A mass of comparative data is also available in Michael Mulhall's enormous *Dictionary of Statistics*, first published in 1895.

Transportation records

Material on transport undertakings tends to be, by its nature, relatively accessible. It is possible, for instance, to know a great deal about a railway company without having access to its private records. After all, it depended on public share issue for its capital and on timetables and advertising to sell its services. Large-scale maps can also given a detailed picture of the capital equipment of the concern—tracks, stations and associated buildings, engine and carriage sheds, etc. The secondary literature on railways is immense, though of variable quality.

The serious study by economic and social historians of the impact of the railway is of very recent date, and the work of historians like G. R. Hawke, *Railways and Economic Growth in England and Wales* (Oxford, 1970) has forced a reappraisal of the whole tradition of railway history, hitherto substantially dominated by the enthusiast and the engineer. This has resulted in an upward revaluation of much of the early writing on railways, 'classic' company histories like W. W. Tomlinson's *North Eastern Railways* (Reid, 1915) and Edward MacDermott's *Great Western Railway* (GWR, 1927–31) and, most notably, of the economic studies of Dionysius Lardner, whose *Railway Economy* (1850) tended to be underrated by writers obsessed with rolling-stock and engineering to the exclusion of economic factors.

Canals have in many ways been better served by historians than railways, notably in the well-documented regional

studies originated, and substantially written by, Charles Hadfield. However, as they were less subject to government supervision than the railways, statistical information on their operation is more difficult to come by. Reprints of two comprehensive source books, straddling the Victorian period, are, luckily, cheaply available: Joseph Priestley's *Historical Account of the Navigable Rivers, Canals and Railways throughout Great Britain* (1831) and Henry Rodolph de Salis's *Bradshaw's Guide to the Inland Waterways of England* (1905).

Road enterprises are the most puzzling of the lot; a great deal of information is available on such of them as were taken into public ownership, like municipal tramway and bus concerns (cf. the *Annual Reports* of such undertakings and minutes of their supervisory committees) but information on coach services and private tramway and bus companies is subject to the same problems of accessibility as other industrial records.

The major archive for transport sources is that of the former *British Transport Commission* at 66 Porchester Road, W2, and the Scottish Record Office, Edinburgh (covering the records of all the concerns nationalized since 1947—railways, canals, bus companies, etc.). The standard source for railway history is George Ottley, *A Bibliography of British Railway History* (Allen & Unwin, 1965). The two main journals in this field are *Transport History* (David & Charles) and *The Journal of Transport History* (Leicester University).

Paper 5: A Guide to Bibliographies, Sources and Collections of Primary Documents

Anthony Coulson

Whilst earlier authors have stressed vital research techniques in this paper I wish to concentrate on some reference works that will help you approach and use primary source material. Probably you will not need to draw on a lot of them but they will certainly help make the most economical use of limited research time.

However, before I put up a few signposts to the maze of published and unpublished documents, please bear in mind that primary and secondary materials raise different problems of conservation, organization and so exploitation. Manuscript materials in particular—letters, bills, account books—cannot be treated in the same way as printed documents and critical works which are easier to house and index. In most cases the collections will be separate and you will need one to find the other.

Consequently your search will begin with a look at secondary materials to find out what has been studied and written up and what has been ignored or passed over. Needless to say, the literature here is vast but a number of bibliographies will help pick out the relevant items swiftly and save many hours. As the availability of specific works is variable and my space is limited, I will discuss them by type and example rather than attempt to be comprehensive:

1 National/Universal Bibliographies

The *British National Bibliography* 1950– (compiled from items received by the Copyright Deposit Office of the British Museum) and the *British Humanities Index* 1962, and its predecessor *Subject Index to Periodicals* 1919–61 (based on a wide range of learned journals, weeklies, newspapers) have useful indexes with detailed subject analysis. As they are both very comprehensive and widely available in libraries they make a very useful starting-point. In larger libraries you might get help from the author and subject indexes of the printed catalogues of the largest libraries in the world (*British Museum General Catalogue of Printed Books, National Union Catalog*—based on the Library of Congress; *London Library Catalogue*—based on the private library rich in nineteenth-century and historical literature) although in most cases they will probably reveal more material than you can cope with, unless your enquiry is very specific. Consequently the more helpful may be the:

2 General Modern History Bibliography

These often treat articles together with books to give a more complete picture of what has been and is being written in some detail. Very often they are tucked away as a section of larger works as in

FREWER, Louis B.
Bibliography of historical writings published in Great Britain and Europe 1940–1945. 1947. Oxford.
LANCASTER, Joan C.
Bibliography of historical works issued in the United Kingdom 1946–1956. 1957. Institute of Historical Research.
KELLAWAY, William
Bibliography of historical works issued in the United Kingdom 1957–60. 1962. Institute of Historical Research.
Bibliography of historical works issued in the United Kingdom 1961–1965. 1967. Institute of Historical Research.
Bibliography of historical works issued in the United Kingdom 1965–70. 1972. Institute of Historical Research.

or as part of an annual supplement as in

HISTORICAL ASSOCIATION
Annual Bulletin of Historical Literature 1911– .

The detailed period and topic listings may well give a helpful lead into a related field.

However, if you want a more detailed critical guide to relevant historical writings to give a clearer idea of the relative weight of items written, you will need more detailed annotation together with a survey of the literature as a whole. Here guides to the literature will help:

AMERICAN HISTORICAL ASSOCIATION
Guide to Historical Literature. 1957. American Historical Association.
ROACH, John, editor
A Bibliography of Modern History. 1968. Cambridge (intended to supplement the *New Cambridge Modern History*)
COULTER, Edith M. and GERSTENFELD, Melanie
Historical Bibliographies. A systematic and annotated guide. 1965. Russell & Russell (originally pub. 1935).

The comments and indexes may well open up useful material in an unexpectedly related field. However, this vital cross reference may often be helped by using these works together with a more limited bibliography:

3 Period or Topic Bibliography

Easier to compile and more widely disseminated, this type represents a very rapidly expanding literature in its own right. On the one hand there is the very useful Historical Association *Helps for Students of History* series, which centre on a particular topic, theme or period, e.g.

No. 58 CHRIMES, S. B. and ROOTS, I. A., eds.
English Constitutional History. 1958.
No. 61 MOWAT, C. L.
British History since 1926. 1961.
No. 80 KIRBY, J. L.
A Guide to Historical Periodicals in the English Language. 1970.

Compact, inexpensive and very easy to use. Alternatively you may wish to use the more intricate and detailed listings prepared by the Institute of Historical Research and Royal Historical Society to help you find something more specific:

ROYAL HISTORICAL SOCIETY
Writings on British History 1901–33. 1968– . Jonathan Cape (particularly vols. 4 and 5).
MUNRO, D. J.
Writings on British History 1946–48. 1973 Institute of Historical Research.

or larger specialist bibliographies which may now be rather elderly, e.g.

PARGELLIS, Stanley and MEDLEY, D. J.
Bibliography of British history: the eighteenth century 1714–89. 1959. Oxford.
WILLIAMS, Judith B.
A guide to the printed materials for English Social and Economic History 1750–1850. 1966 Octagon (1st printed 1926).

However, these are best approached after you have a more general picture of the literature you wish to search and this may be conveniently gained either from the works discussed by John Golby and Clive Emsley or:

4 Major English Historical Series

Fortunately these are fairly widely available in all types of libraries, and though their bibliographies are often a bit elderly they may give a useful guide and start:

Cambridge Modern History 1902–26. A series largely superseded by the more modern *New Cambridge Modern History* 1957 or the *Oxford History of England* 1935–65 particularly
WATSON, J. S.
The Reign of George III 1769–1815. 1960. OUP.
WOODWARD, L.
The Age of Reform 1815–1870. 2nd ed. 1962. OUP.
ENSOR, R. C. K.
England 1870–1914, 1936. OUP.
TAYLOR, A. J. P.
English History 1914–1945. 1965. OUP.

or volumes in other large series such as that published by Methuen, e.g.
MOWAT, C. L.
Britain between the Wars 1918–1940. 1955. Methuen.

However, if you want more up-to-date information you will probably need to tackle the lists and reviews in:

5 Historical Periodicals

Most of the major national historical journals dealing with the period that concerns us carry useful review articles, e.g. *American Historical Review, Economic History Review, Journal of Contemporary History* (1966–), *Journal of World History* (1953–), *History, History Today,* although the most useful for up-to-date information and detailed analysis is the *English Historical Review* (1886–) which helpfully has notes on periodical publications in its July issues and a useful cumulated *Annual Supplement.* The reviews are very detailed and give a lot of useful comment.

Apart from the national journals there is an enormous range of journals concerned with more limited fields of history:

(a) Local History

The *Local Historian* (formerly the *Amateur Historian*), a quarterly giving probably the best overall guide to lesser-known writings and studies through its reviews. On a more purely local level there are many journals published by societies, e.g. *Northamptonshire Past and Present, Manchester Review,* or by history, adult education and extra-mural departments of universities, e.g. *Bulletin of Local History, East Midland Region* (University of Nottingham), *Northern History* (University of Leeds). Nearly always they will be the most up-to-date sources of information particularly when taken with journals concerned with:

(b) History of a specific subject or field

e.g. *Transport History, Textile History, Bulletin of the Society for the Study of Labour History.*

The main problem is the number and ever increasing range but perhaps the best way of finding out the relevant journals is to try to identify the scope of your subject and see which societies, local and national, operate in that area and then find out what they publish. Your local reference librarian will be able to help you here.

Alternatively you might be fortunate enough in a larger library to be able to use *Historical Abstracts 1775–1945, a Bibliography of the World*'s *Periodical Literature* (published by Clio) in which you will find detailed summaries of relevant articles after consulting the full indexes.

In many cases these local or specialized periodicals will provide you with a great amount of really up-to-date bibliographical information though this is variable. Along with the state of the *Victoria County Histories* and local publications in general they vary from area to area, and a bit of local knowledge such as that provided by your local library can be a great help. However, these periodicals will generally provide you with useful comment and information often in advance of the larger journals and books.

Also they provide a useful bridgehead to primary materials if you are unable to dig into the largely unpublished world of theses, detailed in ASLIB *Index of Theses* or now fully indexed in

LONDON UNIVERSITY. Institute of Historical Research *Annual List of historical research for university degrees in the United Kingdom.* 1931– . Part 1—Theses Completed. Part 2—Theses in Progress.

Don't be frightened by the details of all these books many of which you will not need or want to use. It's useful to know they exist, as they may be able to help you if you get stuck or want to break into a field unknown to you at present. The same is even more true of the comments that follow on books to help you tackle primary source material.

Sources and Collections of Primary Documents

Before diving into unpublished and other primary sources stop and ask three questions:

1 What is the precise nature of the material I am looking for?
2 Where is it?
3 How can I get hold of it?

The area in front of you is vast, often unknown or charted in ways that may be unusual and difficult to understand. Consequently please treat the following works as possible signposts and clues to help you answer these basic questions.

A lot of these books are now unfortunately out of print or only obtainable in the largest libraries or repositories, but I hope you will find it helpful to know of the existence of guides and lists in planning research even if you will ultimately only use a fairly small number of them.

Remember that the author of most national, local and business documents is rarely a person but usually a department or agency. This may seem self-evident but this is the reason most repositories reproduce the administrative structure in their organization of classes of documents. Consequently, subject approaches can only be made through scanning guides and calendars where available. However, there are vast ranges uncatalogued, and the best way of finding a point of entry is through a careful study of secondary sources, such as the *Victoria County Histories,* to build up your knowledge of local and national structures. This should suggest administrative activities worth investigating and this is where you may find some of the following works useful in working out how these were administered and recorded.

Many thousands of primary documents are to be found in the most extraordinary places as a result of sale, theft, neglect, flood and all manner of human decision and chance. Inevitably this makes finding them a matter of luck as well as judgement, but you can help make your searches more precise if you can work out fairly exactly the function of the record, who issued it and to whom, and which officials were involved. This may well give you a vital clue as a lot of official documents have strayed into private hands. Even in the nineteenth century important official documents might be retained in the private papers of Prime Ministers and other senior officials. As most of the smaller archives have grown up as a result of local enthusiasm for particular local figures, events and places and still reflect these particular interests, this may well suggest where to start looking. However, there are two pamphlets that may be worth while buying and keeping by your side in your travels and searches if you need to touch the unpublished:

EMMISON, F. G. and SMITH, W. J.
Material for Theses in some Local Record Offices 1973. Phillimore; and

CLARK, George Kitson and ELTON G. R.
Guide to research facilities in history in the universities of Great Britain and Ireland. 1965. Cambridge University Press.

Both are inexpensive and have a lot of useful information provided by the institutions concerned.

Before setting off for any archive collection please bear in mind that using primary documents is a very lengthy and exacting business and a high degree of advance planning and preparation will make a great difference to the efficiency and accurate results of your visits. Consequently try to work out in advance:

1 Records in print—if records have been printed you will very often find it more convenient to consult them elsewhere, particularly in libraries.

2 Classes and types of documents that need to be searched.

3 Accessibility—how to gain admission, times of opening, restrictions on documents. (A lot of family and modern official records may not be available to the researcher at all and it is best to find this out in advance.)

In any case you should contact curators of the documents you wish to consult a good time before your visit to identify and overcome any initial and local problems.

Bearing all this in mind I hope you will find some useful leads in one of the following sections:

1 Documents in print

a General Collections in Print—a select list
b Government Publications
c Regional and Local Records
d Family and Business Records

2 Manuscript and unpublished records

a Repositories
b Migration of Archives
c Local History and Record Societies
d Guides to Particular Types of Records

1 Documents in Print

a General Collections in Print

In the last fifteen years a great many collections of original documents (ranging from the 1000 volume Irish University Press reprint of select *British Parliamentary Papers* to modest paperbacks) have appeared. Many of these have had wide circulation and you might find it helpful to turn up some of these in your local library or bookshop:

(i) Spanning most of the period

BAGLEY, (J. J.)	Historical interpretation, 2: Sources of English history 1540 to the present day	1971	Penguin
BARKER, W. A. and other editors	Documents of English history 1688–1832; edited by W. A. Barker, G. R. St.Aubyn and R. L. Ollard	1964	Black
BARKER, W. A. and other editors	Documents of English history 1832–1950; edited by W. A. Barker, G. R. St.Aubyn and R. L. Ollard	1964	Black
COSTIN, W. C. and WATSON, J. S. *eds.*	The Law and the Constitution documents 1660–1914		
	Vol. 1: 1660–1783	1961	Black
	Vol. 2: 1784–1914	1964	Black
EVANS, Lloyd, and PLEDGER, P. J. compilers	Contemporary sources and opinions in modern British history (2 vols.)	1967	F. Warne
HORN, D. B. *ed.*	English historical documents 1714–1815	1967	Methuen
	English historical documents 1815–1870	1964	Methuen
JACKMAN, S. W. *ed.*	English reform tradition 1790–1910		Spectrum
LANE, P. *ed.*	Documents in British economic and social history (3 vols.)	1968–9	Macmillan
	1: 1750–1870		
	2: 1870–1939		
	3: 1939–		
PLEDGER, P. J. and EVANS, L.	Contemporary sources and opinions in modern British history (2 vols.)	1968	Warne
SCHUYLER, R. L. and WESTON, C. C. *eds.*	Cardinal documents in British history	1961	Anvil
STEPHENSON, Carl and MARCHAM, George F.	Sources of English constitutional history	1937	Harper & Row
CHARLES-EDWARDS, T. and RICHARDSON, B. compilers	They saw it happen: an anthology of eye-witnesses' accounts of events in British history (vol. 3) 1689–1897	1958	Blackwell
BRIGGS, Asa compiler	They saw it happen: an anthology of eye-witnesses' accounts of events in British history (vol. 4) 1897–1940	1960	Blackwell
WILLS, Geoffrey	The English life series:	1968	Exeter: Wheaton
	Vol. 4: 1760–1820		
	Vol. 5: 1820–1855		
	Vol. 6: 1855–1900		

WROUGHTON, John	Documents in British political history: Book 1: 1688–1815 Book 2: 1815–1914	1971	Macmillan

(ii) Periods

(a) Mainly Eighteenth Century

HORN, D. B. and RANSOME, M. *eds.*	English historical documents Vol. 10: 1714–1783	1957	Eyre & Spottiswoode
ASPINALL, A. and ANTHONY SMITH, E. *eds.*	English historical documents Vol. 11: 1783–1832	1959	Eyre & Spottiswoode
HORN, D. B., *ed.*	English historical documents 1714–1815, Vols. X and XI Selection . . .	1967	Methuen
BRIGGS, A. compiler	How they lived: Anthology of original documents written between 1700 and 1815 (Vol. 3)	1969	Blackwell
MILLWARD, J. S. and ARNOLD-CRAFT, H. P. *eds.*	The Eighteenth Century 1714–1783	1962	Hutchinson
REESE, M. M.	British history 1688–1815	1971	Arnold
WILLIAMS, E. N. *ed.*	The Eighteenth Century Constitution, documents and commentary 1688–1815·	1960	Cambridge

(b) Mainly Nineteenth Century

BLACK, E. C.	British politics in the Nineteenth Century	1969	Harper & Row
DAWSON, K. and WALL, P. *eds.*	Society and industry in the 19th Century: a documentary approach (6 vols.) Vol. 1 Parliamentary representation 1968 Vol. 2 Factory reform 1968 Vol. 3 Trade unions 1968 Vol. 4 Education 1969 Vol. 5 Problem of poverty 1969 Vol. 6 Public Health and Housing 1971	1968/9	Oxford
DE VRIES, L.	Panorama 1842 to 1865: The world of the early Victorians as seen through the eyes of the *Illustrated London News*	1967	Murray
DONCASTER, I.	Changing society in Victorian England 1850–1900 (Evidence in Pictures series)	1966	Longmans
YOUNG, E. M. and HANDCOCK, W. D. *eds.*	English historical documents Vol. 12(1): 1833–1874	1956	Eyre & Spottiswoode
	English historical documents 1815–1870: being a selection of documents from 'English historical documents' vols. XI and XII(1)	1964	Methuen
HANHAM, H. J. *ed.*	The 19th Century Constitution 1815–1914: documents and commentary	1969	Oxford
HOLMAN, D.	The earlier 19th Century 1783–1867	1965	Hutchinson
KAUVAR, G. B.	The Victorian mind: an anthology	1970	Cassell in assc'n. with Vic. Society
LAZARUS, M. E.	Victorian social conditions and attitudes 1837–71 (Sources of History series)	1969	Macmillan
LEVINE, G. L. compiler	The emergence of Victorian consciousness: the new spirit of the age	1967	Collier- Macmillan
ELLIS, Sir Henry (notes and illustrations by)	Original letters illustrative of English history, including numerous royal letters from autographs in the British Museum, the State Paper Office and one or two other collectors; 11 vols.	1969	Dawsons
PIKE, E. R. *ed.*	Human documents of the Victorian golden age (1850–1875)	1966	Allen & Unwin
CREWE, Quentin	The frontiers of privilege: a century of social conflict as reflected in *The Queen*	1961	Collins
SNYDER, L. L.	Fifty major documents of the 19th Century	1955	Anvil
TEED, P. and CLARK, M. *eds.*	The later 19th Century 1868–1919	1969	Hutchinson
TREMLETT, T. D.	British history 1815–1914	1971	E. Arnold

(c) Mainly Twentieth Century

BETTY, J. H. compiler	English historical documents 1906–1939	1967	Routledge & Kegan Paul

BRITISH MUSEUM	The political scene 1901–1914: an exhibition to commemorate the 50th anniversary of the Parliament Act 1911.	1961	British Museum
CLARK, M. and TEED, P.	The 20th Century 1906–1960	1971	Hutchinson
DELGADO, A.	Edwardian England: illustrated from contemporary sources	1967	Longmans
EDES, M. E. and FRASER, D. eds.	The age of extravagance: an Edwardian reader	1955	Weidenfeld & Nicolson
HARRISON, M. and ROYSTON, O. M.	Picture source book for social history: the 20th Century	1967	Unwin
LAVER, J. compiler	Edwardian promenade	1958	Hulton Press
LEMAY, G. H. L. ed.	British government 1914–53: select documents	1955	Methuen
PIKE, E. R.	Human documents of the age of the Forsytes	1969	Allen & Unwin
SYNDER, L. L.	Fifty major documents of the 20th Century	1955	Anvil

(iii) Topics

BLAND, A. E., BROWN, P. A. and TAWNEY, R. H.	English economic history: select documents	1914 reprint 1937	Bell
	Focal aspects of the Industrial Revolution 1825–1842	1971	Irish UP
PIKE, E. R. compiler	Human documents of the Industrial Revolution in Britain	1966	Allen & Unwin
TAMES, R. L.	Documents of the Industrial Revolution 1750–1850 Vol. 1: Expanding economy Vol. 2: The social impact	1971	Hutchinson
TRANTER, N. L. ed.	Population and industrialisation	1972	Black
PARK, J. H. ed.	British Prime Ministers of the 19th Century: policies and speeches	1951	New York UP
GRINTER, R.	Disraeli and Conservatism	1968	Arnold
ROOKE, P. J.	Gladstone and Disraeli (Wayland Documentary History series)	1970	Wayland Publishers
SEAMAN, R. D. H.	The Reform of the Lords	1971	Arnold
EVANS, L. W.	British trade unionism 1850–1914	1970	Arnold
LENIN, V. I.	British labour and British imperialism: a compilation of writings by Lenin on Britain	1969	Lawrence & Wishart
LEWIS, R. A.	Public health in 19th Century Britain	1970	Arnold
MARX-ENGELS-LENIN-STALIN INSTITUTE, Moscow	Karl Marx and Frederick Engels on Britain Contents: The constitution of the working class in England (Engels); Articles on Britain, by Marx & Engels; Letters on Britain by Engels & Marx	1954	Moscow Foreign Language Press
MAYHEW, H.	London labour and the London poor: selected by John L. Bradley	1965	Oxford
PLACE, F.	London Radicalism 1830–43: a selection from the papers of Francis Place, edited by D. J. Row	1970	Inst. of Historical Research
MANCHESTER PUBLIC LIBRARIES	Peterloo 1819: a portfolio of contemporary documents	1969	Manchester PL
FFRENCH, Y. ed.	Translatic exchanges: cross currents of Anglo-American opinion in the 19th Century: selected and introduced by Yvonne Ffrench	1951	Sidgwick & Jackson
JAMES, M.	The emancipation of women in Great Britain	1971	Arnold

---

However, these include only the most important and accessible documents and, particularly if you do not have access to *British Parliamentary Papers* (which include a lot of valuable supporting evidence and reports), you may find the two British Records Association publications

SOMERVILLE, R
Handlist of record publications. 1951. British Records Association pamphlet No. 3 and its complement
GOULDSBROUGH, F. and others
Handlist of Scottish and Welsh record publications. 1954. British Records Association pamphlet No. 4

useful in their listing of administrative groups and the type and titles of documents generated.

Many of these documents are published in series or subsequently listed by Record or other research societies who also undertake detailed listings and descriptions of their form and chronology. Here the analytical entries of

MULLINS, Edward Lindsay Carson
Texts and calendars: an analytical guide to serial publications. 1958. Royal Historical Society (Guides and Handbooks No. 7)

may be found helpful in its wide coverage of official series (e.g. Historical Manuscripts Reports) and important independent 'unofficial' bodies (e.g. English Historical Society).

(b) Government Publications

The documents generated and published by central government and its departments constitute the largest and most complex bodies of documents.

Every year the government prints what are called the Sessional or Parliamentary Papers. These can be roughly divided into three categories: the reports of Civil Service departments, the reports of Select Committees of both Houses, and the reports of specially appointed Royal Commissions. They constitute the largest single source of printed information on British society in the nineteenth and twentieth centuries and have been ceaselessly quarried by historians from Karl Marx on. It has been argued that rather too much reliance has been placed on them, as they tend to concentrate on what was going wrong with society and that Royal Commissions in particular were impartial bodies with a definite reforming aim in mind. This is certainly true of some of the post-1832 Commissions, like those into the Poor Law and Municipal Corporations, but it is less true of later nineteenth-century commissions, like that of 1884 into working-class housing, which contains a vast amount of information, even now little used by historians. However, to help find your way through the daunting and often confusing bulk of these records a number of larger libraries have published their own guides which help make their collections easier to use. Two examples are:

UNIVERSITY OF ESSEX LIBRARY
Reference Leaflet No. 1 British Government Publications. 1971.
BIRMINGHAM UNIVERSITY LIBRARY
A Directory of British Government Publications. 1966.

The latter goes right to the heart of one of the major problems of dealing with these printed items—confusing terminology and inaccurate description—which I expect you will have noticed as a sin perpetuated by a lot of secondary sources.

Perhaps this is inevitable with large bodies spanning the 200 years of our field of interest, but a good way to arm yourself is to understand and find out how the publications are ordered, created and used. Two recent monographs on contemporary British government publications are particularly useful here and should be widely available:

OLLÉ, James G
An Introduction to British Government Publications, 1973 (2nd ed.)
Association of Assistant Librarians.
PEMBERTON, John
British Official Publications, 1971. Pergamon.

Certainly legislative practices, and so documents, have changed over 200 years but the insight (e.g. Pemberton pp. 73–87 on the function and creations of Royal Commissions) these books give into the structure, function and value of the publications is very useful. In a similar way with its concentration in separate chapters on individual departments of government

STAVELEY, Ronald, and PIGGOTT, Mary
Government Information and the research worker. 1965. Library Association

adds a lot of useful comment and data on practices within particular areas written by information workers from those areas.

Whilst these books can help identify the sort of documents to be searched the next problem is to sort out what is now available in published form. Fortunately the index publications of Her Majesty's Stationery Office are a great help:

Sectional List 24: British National Archives (gratis on application to HMSO)

Includes all official Record publications whether in print or not (many of the older documents are being reprinted by the Kraus–Thomson Organisation Limited). Record publications are here understood as publications of the Public Record Office, House of Lords Record Office, Record Commissioners, Scottish Record Office, Northern Ireland Record Office, Scottish Record Office. Taken with

Sectional List 17: Publications of the Royal Commission on Historical Manuscripts (gratis on application to HMSO)

these frequently updated lists cover all the reproduced documents, guides and indexes published by central government *record* agencies.

However, with documents published by central government and its agencies in the normal course (as distinct from those republished by the official record agencies) you will find the HMSO

Annual Catalogue of Publications
covers publications year by year since it started publication in 1922. As both this annual volume and the Sectional Lists have detailed indexes it is possible to hunt up useful material from a subject approach (given a store of synonyms and detail references).

Acts and other statutory instruments still in force can be seen in

HALSBURY, Earl
Statutes of England. Butterworth (41 vols.)
which with its detailed subject index might well make a useful point of departure for more localised studies or investigations of legislative activities during particular periods. A less detailed listing of all Public General Acts whether or not still in force is contained in

STATUTORY PUBLICATIONS OFFICE
Chronological Table of Statutes to the end of 1970, 1971 HMSO.

However, beyond the materials listed by these indexes lies a vast range of publications some of which are now being reprinted. With the Irish Universities Press republication of a very full selection of parliamentary papers in their 1000 volume series *British Parliamentary Papers 1800–1899* there is now a much better chance of investigating this primary source in larger libraries. The best way of approaching this series is through its index *Checklist of British Parliamentary Papers* with separate indexes covering chronology, subject and keyword title. The series is also splendidly explained in its accompanying volume

FORD, P. and G.
A Guide to Parliamentary Papers 1972 Irish Universities Press.

Taken with the other indexes of parliamentary papers which you still may be able to see in larger and older libraries:

HANSARD, J. and L.
Catalogue and Breviate of Parliamentary Papers 1696–1834, 1834

KING, P. S.
Catalogue of Parliamentary Papers 1801–1900, 1914
(with its irritating lack of reference to numbers of papers or volumes)

FORD, P. and G.
Select List of British Parliamentary Papers 1833–99. 1969. Irish Universities Press
A Breviate of Parliamentary Papers 1900–16. 1969. Irish Universities Press
A Breviate of Parliamentary Papers 1917–39. 1969. Irish Universities Press
A Breviate of Parliamentary Papers 1940–50. 1969. Irish Universities Press

and to cover the gap

HANSARD, Luke Graves
Diary 1814–41, ed. P. and G. Ford. 1962. Blackwell

it should be possible to pinpoint the documents required in this corpus with considerable accuracy.

If, however, this range of indexes is not available to you, scanning *Hansard* during the required period may help you approach this material provided that you remember that it has only been the official organ of report with special staff since 1909. Between 1803 and 1909 reporting was in the private hands of the Cobbett and Hansard families and before then reporting was patchy and generally semi-official. Speeches are reported verbatim but in the third person, and are subject to post-debate alterations by the speakers. The volumes (up to five or six a session) are indexed cumulatively—i.e. the last volume of the session covers all preceding ones, and are indexed both by subjects and speakers. In books and theses references are usually given thus: Speech of Lord Palmerston on University Reform in *Hansard* (or *Parliamentary Debates*) 3s clxx, 1240. 3s means third series—a new series opened with every reign. clxx indicates the 170th volume of the series (in this case for 1863) and 1240 is the *column* number (*Hansard* was printed in double-column). Division lists are given, but not MPs' politics (these can be found out by consulting the annual copy of *Dod's Parliamentary Companion* or *McCalmont's Parliamentary Poll Book* (1910, reprinted Harvester Press, 1971).

As you may find original parliamentary papers scattered in library collections you may also come upon some of the following older or more specialized indexes that may help you search out useful printed material:

RODGERS, Frank
Serial Publications in the British Parliamentary Papers 1900–1968: a bibliography. 1971. Library Association.

POWELL, W. R.
Local History from Blue Books: a select list of the Sessional Papers of the House of Commons. 1962. Historical Association (Helps for History Students).
Reports from Committees of the House of Commons 1715–1801 (15 vols.).

General Index to the House of Commons 1715–1801. 1803.
General Index to the Reports of Select Committees 1801–1852. 1853.
General Index to the Accounts and Papers, Reports of Commissioners, Estimates etc., 1801–1852. 1853
General Index to the Bills 1801–1852. 1853.
General alphabetical index to the Bills, Reports and Estimates, Accounts and Papers 1852–1899. 1909.
General Index to the Bills, Reports and Papers . . . and to Reports and Papers presented by Command 1900–1948/9. 1960.

One problem you will find with some of these indexes and also with isolated original documents associated with parliamentary papers is the numbering. However, if you remember that House of Commons papers are numbered by session and that Command Papers for our period are in five series:

1–4222	(1833 to 1868/9)
C1–C9550	(1870 to 1899)
Cd1–Cd9239	(1900 to 1918)
Cmd1–Cmd9889	(1919 to 1955/6)

any other problems relate to chronology that can swiftly be solved by referring to

CHENEY, C. R.
Handbook of dates for students of English History. 1961. Royal Historical Society
or
POWICKE, F. M. and FRYDE, L. B.
Handbook of British Chronology 1961 (2nd ed.) Royal Historical Society.

I hope this list is not too daunting, particularly if I add that it is very selective and ignores many large problems. However, if you feel you have to work extensively on parliamentary records either at Westminster or elsewhere you will find the book by the Archivist of the House of Lords Records Office

BOND, Maurice F.
Guide to the Records of Parliament. 1971. HMSO.

immensely useful. He both describes the complete range of records preserved in the Palace of Westminster (including papers accumulated in the various Parliamentary and non-Parliamentary offices, printed and manuscript) as well as providing very helpful notes and accounts of their history, function and nature. With a detailed index and full bibliographies it is at once a very valuable guide to an immensely rich collection and one of the most important bibliographies of Parliamentary records.

(c) Regional and Local Records in Print

With local and regional records the pressure and need to publish is not as strong and so I discuss books dealing with the types of records and collections in the second half of the paper with manuscript and unpublished resources. Those that are printed often form part of series or collections to commemorate a particular event or show off the resources of a particular collection, e.g.

MELLING, Elizabeth, editor
Kentish Sources III Aspects of Agriculture and Industry. A collection of examples from original sources in the Kent Archives Office, from the sixteenth century to the nineteenth century. 1961. Kent CC.

Consequently the best ways of locating and identifying them are by checking

1 Publications lists of the local County Record Office.

2 Publications lists of the local record or archaeological or historical society.

3 Publications lists of national learned societies that may have a special interest in the topic being researched (e.g. Economic History Society or Railway and Canal Historical Society)—the addresses of the societies with details of aims and policy can be obtained from the latest editions of *Whitaker's Almanack* and the British Council's *Scientific and Learned Societies of Great Britain*.

4 County Bibliographies—there are now many available that have been prepared with very considerable bibliographical skill and detail, e.g.

CONISBEE, L. R.
A Bedfordshire bibliography
Older bibliographies are indexed and annotated occasionally in

HUMPHREYS, Arthur Lee
Handbook to county bibliography; being a bibliography . . .
1917. Strangeways.

5 Local histories—useful books for tracing these are:
GROSS, Charles
A Bibliography of British Municipal History. 1897. Longmans (reprinted).
LIBRARY ASSOCIATION
Reader's Guide to books on the sources of local history.
1964 (3rd ed.). Library Association.
KUHLICKE, F. W. and EMMISON, F. G. editors
English local history handlist. 1969 (4th ed.).
Historical Association (Helps for Students of History no. 69).

6 Local History Collection of the local Public Library or Museum—very often for their own internal uses they have detailed indexes covering all kinds of primary material in their collections or in locality. Also useful point of information for publications planned for the future and currently being researched/edited.

Parish records that have been printed are best sought out in this way, although if you wish to trace copies of Parish Registers you will find helpful

SOCIETY OF GENEALOGISTS
Parish Register Copies:
1 *In Society of Genealogists Collection.* 1970 (3rd ed.).
Phillimore.
2 *Other than the Society of Genealogists Collection.*
1970. Phillimore.

(d) Business and Family Records

As well as using the lines of approach suggested for turning up local records these publications are often best brought to the surface by published diaries, biographies and company histories. In digging these up you may find useful:

MATTHEWS, W. compiler
British diaries; an annotated bibliography of British diaries written between 1442 and 1942. 1950. Cambridge UP.

HANHAM, H. J.
Some neglected sources of biographical information: county biographical dictionaries 1800–1937, pp. 55–66 *Bulletin of the Institute of Historical Research*, vol. 34, no. 89, May 1961.

MATTHEWS, William
British Autobiographies. Annotated bibliography of British autobiographies published or written before 1951. 1968.
Archon Books.

Ancient family and commercial conflicts will then often lead to the County Record Office and its legal records.

2 Manuscript and Unpublished Records

As most of your research efforts are likely to be concentrated on local archives I will concentrate in this part of the paper on

1 Repositories—their nature, published guides and how to find them.
2 Local History, Records Societies and how to find them.
3 Unpublished records and helps to deal with them.

(a) Repositories

Most record collections have grown up as a result of haphazard decisions rather than a centrally conceived plan as in France. Consequently not only do collections of the same type differ radically in organization and contents but the types of material deposited are often dependent on decisions elsewhere. For instance, government department records are deposited at the Public Record Office at the discretion of the donor and so records of some departments (or former departments), e.g. Post Office and Forestry Commission are not there at all. These complications can often restrict access both to family and business records as well as modern public affairs records. Consequently this may need to be investigated at an early stage.

Fortunately all major systematically organized collections are listed in

ROYAL COMMISSION ON HISTORICAL MANUSCRIPTS
Record repositories in Great Britain. 1973 (5th ed.). HMSO.
50p.

In very compact form it details addresses, telephone numbers and names to contact together with brief information as to guides published, times and conditions under which the collection can be used.

These tend to fall into these main categories:

(i) *Public Records Offices*

i.e. records of Parliament, central government departments, courts of law. Some preserve all papers for reference but as most are transferred to the Public Record Office, Scottish Record Office, Public Record Office of Northern Ireland, they are best approached through the guides and lists of these institutions:

PUBLIC RECORD OFFICE
Guide to the Public Records. Part 1 Introductory. 1949.
HMSO.
Guide to the Manuscripts Preserved in the Public Record Office by M. S. Giuseppi.
Vol. 1 Legal Records, 1923. HMSO.

Vol. 2 State Papers, etc. 1924. HMSO.
Guide to the Contents of the Public Record Office
Vol. 1 Legal Records, etc. 1963. HMSO.
Vol. 2 State Papers and Departmental Records. 1963. HMSO.
Vol. 3 Documents transferred to the Public Record Office 1960–1966. 1969. HMSO.
(these 3 volumes superseded Giuseppi's *Guide*)

LIVINGSTONE, M.
Guide to the Public Records of Scotland deposited in H.M. General Register House Edinburgh. 1905. Edinburgh: General Register House and

ANGUS, W.
Accessions to the Public Records in Register House since 1905, Scottish Historical Review, vol. 26, no. 101, April 1947. pp. 26–46.

WOOD, H.
Guide to the Records in the Public Record Office, Ireland. 1920. HMSO.

PUBLIC RECORD OFFICE OF NORTHERN IRELAND
Catalogues and Guides, no. 1. HMSO.

BOND, M. F.
Guide to the Records of Parliament. 1971. HMSO.

All have very useful descriptions of the documents contained which will help identify the required classes and papers which can be searched out by using the many shelf lists, handbooks and calendars published by them or by the List and Index Society (PRO Shelf lists).

(ii) Local Record Offices

Concerned primarily with local authority records but contents and organization vary considerably:

1 County Record Offices

Collections centre on local records of county administration and jurisdiction together with public records of local origin (Quarter Sessions, Coroner's Courts) together with a variable number of items relating to county or country affairs often from family or estate records. Most publish/aim to publish/have a guide of sorts occasionally with ambitious publication programmes. There are no CROs in Scotland or Northern Ireland and the National Library of Wales undertakes most of these duties for Cardigan, Montgomery and Radnor.

2 City and Borough Record Offices

All are independent and their contents and organization depends very largely on local authority interest. Often this function has been transferred to the local public library, e.g. in Sheffield:

(iii) Libraries, Museums, Archaeological and Antiquarian Societies

Very often these have collections of under 1000 items and, lacking the official status of the respositories already described, can often be difficult to find. Perhaps the best line of approach is to scan

HOBBS, J. L.
Local History and the Library, rev. by George A. Carter. 1973. Deutsch
and

HEPWORTH, P.
Archives and Manuscripts in libraries 1964 Library Association

to search out possible areas, types of documents and published catalogues and guides and then consult the local knowledge of your local reference librarian or county records officer.

(iv) Archives of Religious Bodies

Most Anglican Diocesan Records are now concentrated in CROs or collections of the Dean and Chaper of particular cathedrals. The range of types of record is considerable and if you need to use these collections the pamphlet

OWEN, Dorothy M.
The Records of the Established Church in England excluding Parochial Records 1970 British Records Association (Archives and the User no. 1)

is very helpful in giving you an idea of the sort of material involved. Catholic records remain the responsibility of the presiding bishop whilst Jewish and Non-conformist records are more centralized and the best way of finding the relevant documents is to apply direct to the central agency. The same is true of the resources of the various missionary societies that were so important in the nineteenth century.

(v) Parish Records

In many ways the backbone of information relating to local administration early in the period under study. Many are now deposited in CROs, but same may still be held locally or in private collections. An intriguing but often confusing range of documents; and if you wish to search then have a look at the very lively discussion of the wide range of sorts of documents (maps, registers, etc.) in

TATE, W. E.
The Parish Chest. A study of the Records of Parochial Administration in England. 1969 (3rd ed.). Cambridge.

(vi) Public non-government Bodies

Chris Harvie has already touched on the range of transportation records. Similar vast collections exist for other industries and groups now nationalized, e.g. National Coal Board, British Steel Corporation. Most are in the process of massive reorganization and access is best sought by applying direct.

(vii) Business Archives

The oldest established archives are those of banking and insurance companies, but increasingly larger manufacturing companies, particularly chemical, pharmaceutical and tobacco, are building up systematic archives. Often these contain a lot of very interesting information relating to political or other personalities associated with them at any time. The *Business Archives Council Journal* has surveyed several of these. Unfortunately a lot of material covering smaller firms if not detailed in a company history may still exist in a disorganized state in company cellars, unless it has been deposited at a local CRO in family papers. In all cases best lines of approach are to apply to the company concerned, the local CRO, and the Business Archives Council, 37 Tooley Street, London. S.E.1, with its magnificent collection of Business histories.

(viii)   *Schools, Universities and Colleges*

Most of these are private collections only accessible under certain conditions. However, by far the richest and best organized are the university collections which have been summarized in the very handy pamphlet

CLARK, George Kitson, and ELTON, G. R.
Guide to research facilities in history in the universities of Great Britain and Ireland. 1965. Cambridge University Press.

The resources information is based on that supplied by the institutions, and concentrates on
a   Areas they regard as being specially qualified for research
b   Details of local libraries and their relevant specialities
c   Manuscript collections available
d   Microfilm collections held
e   Who to contact for further detailed enquiries
Another useful introduction to historical education materials is

HIGSON, C. W. J.
Sources for the history of education. 1967. Library Association (with supplements).

(b)   Migration of Archives

Details have so far been given of the repositories that have a reasonably firm and durable foundation. However, many of the sorts of records that you may wish to consult, particularly those in private hands, may have moved as a result of sale, bankruptcy, death, etc. The work of the Royal Commission on Historical Manuscripts has been particularly valuable here through its publications and its two registers:

Reports—over 200 volumes have been published of surveys of collections of privately owned records, mostly pre-1830 and excluding estate records and documents of title but with very useful indexes of places and persons.

National Register of Archives. List of Accessions . . .—an annual volume published since 1958 listed by repository and types of document deposited.

National Register of Archives—a collection in London of over 14,500 typed and duplicated reports on archives some of which have been made into subject source lists on business history, architecture, fine and applied arts and are obtainable from
National Register of Archives,
The Royal Commission on Historical Manuscripts,
Quality House,
Quality Court,
Chancery Lane,
London, WC2A 1HP.

Unfortunately, most of the published guides detailed in *Sectional List 17* are now out of print.
Before 1958 accessions to archives were listed in:
1923–53 Bulletin of the Institute of Historical Research.
1954–56 National Register of Archives Bulletin.

The Institute of Historical Research still lists the migrations of manuscript material on the basis of information acquired from booksellers' and auctioneers' lists.

The work of the National Register is supplemented in Scotland by the efforts of

National Register of Archives (Scotland)
and in the commercial sphere by the efforts of the unofficial
Business Archives Council
Business Archives Council of Scotland.

Also, if you are fortunate enough to be able to consult the two journals *Archives* and *Journal of the Society of Archivists*, you will find that they often deal with recent deposits and new developments and movements in the archives field.

(c)   Local History and Record Societies

Whilst the identity of most of these can be established by consulting *Whitaker's Almanack, Directory of British Associations* and *Scientific and Learned Societies of Great Britain* we are fortunate that there have been some valiant efforts made to index their publications. It is true that the indexes are incomplete and in some cases old but they are very valuable in showing the types of material being published by particular groups and so makes a very useful starting-point for more local and specific enquiries:

YOUINGS, Joyce
Local Record Sources in Print and Progress 1971–2. 1972. Historical Association

MULLINS, E. L. C.
A Guide to the Historical and Archaeological Publications of Societies in England and Wales 1901–1983. 1968. Athlone Press.

TERRY, Charles Sanford
Catalogue of the publications of Scottish historical and kindred clubs and societies, and of the volumes relative to Scottish history issued by H.M.S.O. 1780–1908. 1909. Glasgow: Maclehose.

MATHESON, Cyril
Catalogue of the publications of Scottish . . . 1908–27. 1928. Aberdeen: Milne & Hutchinson.

Local directories will help trace some of the smaller groups, whilst the efforts of the more enterprising will be noticed by some of the national historical journals, e.g. *The Local Historian.*

If you are fortunate enough to locate a sequence of transactions of a relevant local historical or archaeological society do have a careful look at the indexes and check for all possible aspects of the subject you are searching. Very often this will lead you to extremely valuable extracts from original records that may be tucked away in appendices or notes.

(d)   Guides to Particular Types of Records

Even concentrating exclusively on local records it would be possible to fill a number of tomes with a survey of guides and handlists, and so I will concentrate on a few general introductions that will open up particular areas. Most of these books are well known and hopefully still widely available.

Possibly one of the most readable introductions with examples to the whole field of local history studies

EMMISON, F. G.
Archives and Local History. 1966. Longman
contains a very lucid discussion (in Chapter IV *Using Local Archives*, pp. 22–72) of the types of documents most likely to be found and used in local repositories. This

should make a very helpful start particularly if you can then go on to study the slightly more detailed sections on the classes of records in

REDSTONE, L. J. and STEER, F. W. editors
Local Records: their nature and care. 1953. Bell (for Society of Archivists).

The Historical Association has done a lot to help the beginner with different types of document research with its rapidly expanding *Helps for Students of History* series which are inexpensive, concise but directly relevant to needs, e.g.

EMMISON, F. G. and GRAY, Irvine
County Records. 1967 (reprint). Historical Association. H No. 62.

A useful anthology of articles from their journal *History* has been republished:

MUNBY, Lionel M. editor
Short Guides to Records. 1972. Historical Association.

If your searches take you into very specialized areas of documents keep your eyes open for helpful publications by groups and associations, which have been put together for more specialized research in related fields:

CAMP, A. J.
Wills and their whereabouts. 1963. Society of Genealogists.

PURVIS, J. S.
An introduction to Ecclesiastical records. 1953. St Anthony's Press.

HEARNSHAW, F. J. C.
Municipal records. 1918. SPCK.

All have useful clues and background information even though they are designed for students of much more minute and specialized studies than those appropriate to this course.

At first sight the batteries of small-scale local records that can be made available can be frightening, and so you may find it useful to look at two lively and very distinctive books written by enthusiasts who have spent years working over local documents and realize the value of reproducing documents as well as transcriptions and classifications:

WEST, John
Village Records. 1961. Longmans.
TATE, W. F.
The Parish Chest. 1969. (3rd ed.) Cambridge University Press.

Neither are strictly manuals but they give a very clear idea

of how to evaluate and check the accuracy of records by suggesting how records can be used and what they can and cannot reveal.

In particular they are very useful in the way in which they can lead you to little known sources held locally that show the workings of the Poor Law administration through Vestry Books, etc., that may still be in churches or less obvious places.

Finally, do not overlook the importance of purely local physical and economic peculiarities. Ian Donnachie has already discussed how important this is when looking at Industrial Archaeology, but it is often forgotten how much a study of contemporary maps can add to the study of almost all local documents, often giving usful criteria for checking their accuracy and significance. The whole subject is helpfully discussed in

HARLEY, J. B.
Maps for the local historian. A guide to the British sources. 1972. National Council of Social Service

and you may find the following helpful to supplement County Record Office and other local lists:

PUBLIC RECORD OFFICE
Maps and plans in the Public Record Office VI British Isles 1410–1860. 1967. HMSO.

BRITISH MUSEUM
Catalogue of printed maps, charts and plans to 1964. 1967. 15 vols.

FORDHAM, Sir H. G.
The road-books and itineraries of Great Britain 1570–1850. A catalogue. 1924. Cambridge University Press.
Hand-list of catalogues and works of referencc relating to carto-bibliography and kindred subjects for Great Britain and Ireland 1720–1827. 1928. Cambridge U.P.

RODGER, E. M. compiler
Large Scale County Maps of the British Isles 1850–1956. A Union List compiled in the Map section of the Bodleian. 1972. Bodleian.

LEE, J.
English county maps: the identification, cataloguing and physical care of a collection. 1953. Library Association. (Pamphlet 13).

Detailed study of these, coupled with careful field studies, has resulted in the current flowering of local history and studies, as even a casual student of the work of H. P. R. Finberg, M. W. Beresford, A. Everitt, W. G. Hoskins and many others can see.

Grateful acknowledgement is made to the following sources for material used in this block:

J. B. Lowe of the Welsh School of Architecture for illustrations from *Iron Industry Housing Papers No 4; Standard Houses of the First Blaenavon Company, Forge Row, Cwmavon*; W. E. Minchinton and the Department of Economic History, University of Exeter, for illustrations from N. W. Alcock (ed), *Dartington Houses: A Survey*; Dr John Butt, University of Strathclyde, for the print of the cotton mills, reproduced in *Industrial Archaeology of Galloway*, David & Charles, 1971; the Council for British Archaeology.

Great Britain 1750–1950: Sources and Historiography